MOTIVATIONAL INTERVIEWING FOR SCHOOL COUNSELORS

REAGAN A. NORTH

Contents

Foreword 4

Introduction: What Is MI And Why Use It...................6

PART I: EMPATHY...15

Chapter 1: Simple Reflections & Open-Ended Questions 16

Bonus Material 1: How to Be A *Terrible* School Counselor!...........33

Chapter 2: Complex Reflections....................42

Chapter 3: Autonomy & Asking Permission 58

Bonus Material 2: Empathy Checklist...................68

Part II: CHANGE TALK 70

Chapter 4: Change Talk vs. Sustain Talk 71

Chapter 5: Fun with Change Talk! 83

Chapter 6: Responding to Sustain Talk 101

Chapter 7: Commitment & Planning 121

Bonus Material 3: MI Cheat Sheet...................139

Conclusion: You're Changing Lives! 141

Next Steps 143

MI Research...................145

References 147

Foreword

Introductions, Please

Hello, school counselors! My name is Reagan North, and I am a full-time counselor at a great school in Mukilteo, Washington, named Kamiak High School. I've been *slowly* pursuing a PhD on nights and weekends and, along the way, ran across this thing called Motivational Interviewing (MI). After doing some research, I realized 2 things: 1) MI is incredibly powerful, and 2) there is no book out there to train school counselors to use MI. I read several books on MI and spent a bunch of my own money to attend training workshops and receive individualized coaching. After seeing incredible results from using MI with my students, I decided I had to help other school counselors learn to use MI.

Not a Textbook

In my effort to train other school counselors to use MI, I taught a number of workshops at school counseling conferences, introducing the skills to as many people as I could. Along the way, a couple of folks from publishing companies contacted me and asked if I'd write a book on the topic. I was really excited about this! After all, I wanted as many school counselors to learn how to use MI as possible. Sadly, I found out that what the publishing companies really wanted was a textbook. I don't know about you, but I find textbooks to be, well, boring. Since I finished my master's degree and started my career as a school counselor, I can count on one hand the number of times I've consulted an old textbook on one hand.

School Counselors Read, Too

I told the nice folks from the publishing companies that I didn't want to write a textbook; I wanted to write a book that everyday school counselors would want to read, would have the time to read, and would have the money to buy. What I learned was that publishers have to charge a lot of money to make enough profit, and writers have to write a lot of pages to justify the high prices. In other words, they like publishing textbooks for which they can charge big money.

I told the publishers I thought lots of the 300,000+ school counselors in the country would spend time and (less) money to increase their skills, because they care deeply about their students. I proposed they create a line of short, inexpensive books for practicing school counselors. They said "no." They asked me to write a textbook. I said "no." Hence, the self-published book/e-book in your hands.

I'm hoping this book is easy to digest, helpful, and worth your time. I believe in MI, I believe in school counselors, and I believe in our students. Here's to many lives changed for the better!

INTRODUCTION:

What Is MI and Why Use It

School Counseling is Hard!

Being a school counselor is hard. If you are one, you know what I'm talking about.

The American School Counselor Association (2012) recommends that school counselors care for the academic, social-emotional, *and* college-career health of all their students. *Hey, no problem!*

Of course, we school counselors want to care for students in all those areas of life. The problem is that our caseloads are *insane.* ASCA (2012) recommends a student-to-counselor ratio of 250:1. I can hear the laughter from school counselors everywhere as they read that. The average student-to-counselor ratio in the United States is 471:1 (Clark, 2014). In my home state of Washington, it's 510:1 (ASCA, 2011). With such high caseloads and so many students who need our support, we had better be doing things that work. (*Spoiler Alert*: Motivational Interviewing does.)

School counselors are supposed to be sources of healing for their students, but many school counselors are hurting right along with their students. We face crazy expectations given the scope of our jobs and the massive caseloads we serve. Sadly, only 2 out of 10 school counselors believe their master's program prepared them well for the rigors of the profession (The College Board National Office for School Counseling Advocacy, 2011). Imagine how discouraged we'd be if we didn't get paid so extravagantly!

Most school counselors are deeply caring people. We got into the profession because we want to make students' lives better. We spend long hours and emotion-filled days trying to care for the mental health of students. Our students need us, our schools need us, and our communities need us. We can't lose heart. We need tools that will help our students with fiery potency. *(Another Spoiler Alert: Motivational Interviewing does this.)*

Our Students

Because I am a high school counselor by day, I am going to focus much of this book toward those of us who work with adolescents. *Who is that,* you say? Actually, almost all of us. The average age at which children begin puberty is 11 (Clark, 2011). Yes, 11! That means that a significant number of students are hitting puberty in 4th grade. Elementary counselors, you cannot hide from the adolescent hoards!

Why do I even bring up puberty? Some (though not all) of the techniques in this book require that students be able to think abstractly. Children can't really do this until they enter adolescence. If you work with students who are above the 3rd grade, this stuff is GOLD for you. There are plenty of techniques (and an overall mindset) that will work very well with younger children as well. I'll have to rely on the expertise of my elementary counseling colleagues to translate my examples to fit their students below the 4th grade.

Speaking of adolescents, they are in a season of life that will impact the trajectory of their lives like none other. The **bad news** is that teens routinely exhibit higher rates of risky behavior, unprotected sex, and substance use (Park, Mulye, Adams, Brindis, & Irwin, 2006). For many students, negative behaviors that derail them by high school took root in late elementary school and early middle school. The **good news** is that the constant changes occurring in adolescents' lives during this stage make it the perfect time for well-equipped school counselors to help students rip these negative roots out of their souls and point their lives toward beautiful things.

School counselors, you are dangerous. Dangerous for *good!*

Why Be Motivated by Motivation?

Motivational Interviewing (MI), the star of this book, is all about, well, **motivation**! Why does motivation matter? According to MI (and common sense), motivation is the driving force for *all* actions. We do everything because we are motivated to do it. Even when we don't feel motivated to do something - take out the trash, for instance - we are more motivated to run the trash bin to the curb than we are to live in piles of filth.

The same is true of students in our schools. They only do things they are motivated to do. The problem is that our educational system tries to use *external force* to mandate that students change. This external force takes the shape of progressive discipline, suspensions, low grades, calls home, verbal threats, etc. These things may, at best, lead to short-term change. At worst, they run students right out of our schools. Either way, the change is only temporary. Students won't really change unless their hearts are in it.

Enter *Motivational Interviewing.*

What Is Motivational Interviewing?

Here's the best definition of MI I've seen: Motivational Interviewing "is about arranging conversations so that people [students] talk **themselves** into change, based on **their own** values and interests." (Miller & Rollnick, 2013, p. 4; emphases added)

We'll spend the rest of the book talking about how to do MI. For now, notice who is emphasized in this definition - *students*. MI is not a form of counseling that gives people in authority the power to get others to do what they want. MI is about drawing out the *internal* motivations of students. That's why it's so powerful! When you hear that, it might immediately make you nervous since, as someone who works with adolescents every day, you know their internal drives aren't always...awesome. Fear not! MI draws motivation out of students, but it also gives counselors the ability to choose *what* we draw out of them. I'll explain more about this later.

If you boiled MI down to its most basic parts, it would look something like this:

$$MI = Empathy + Change\ Talk$$

If the school counselor *shows* a ton of **empathy** to students and encourages them to talk about why they would want to make a change (**Change Talk**), they are likely to follow through and make a positive change in their lives. We'll spend the next 7 chapters discussing how to do everything we can to make this happen.

What MI-ers Believe

Ambivalence Is Omnipresent. Everyone is ambivalent about something. Actually, according to MI, everyone is ambivalent most of the time. We choose to do certain things because we are more committed to them than not, but decisions are a spectrum.

For those of us who are rooting for students to make good decisions, this is good news! It means that, though students may be making bad choices, it's not because they are destined to do so. In fact, though they are making certain negative decisions, they are also considering the positive alternatives as well. The beauty of MI is that it helps students grow their desire to make the right choice.

Ambivalence is a source of great hope because it means that the most hardened drug dealer, angriest bully, and lowest-scoring student are all thinking about making positive changes in their lives. With MI skills, you can help guide them in the right direction!

People WANT to Be Well. Students (and coworkers, parents, community members, etc.) want to be the best version of themselves. A central belief of MI is that, given the right environment of care, all people naturally tend toward the best outcome. Their souls are pulled toward self-actualization.

Motivational Interviewing is, in part, knowing how to get barriers out of the way so people can become what they are made to be. MI done well throws the doors of students' hearts open and lets the gold flow.

Students First. We use MI because we care about our students and want the best for them. This may sound obvious, but it's important to mention. So much of what goes on in the educational system is based on adult structures trying to force students to do what is "expected of them." MI should *never* be used to get students to do what adults want them to do.

MI exists to help people achieve what they want for *themselves*. This is not a scary proposition because, like we discussed above, when the junk of life is stripped away and students feel comfortable to dream, they want *good* things for themselves. An MI-using school counselor can help students pursue those good things.

Why Use MI? Because It Works!

This is no textbook. You've read enough of those in your life. That being the case, I won't bore you with pages of research supporting MI. The fact that you're reading this book means you think MI is worth learning.

Suffice it to say that MI is one of the hot young stars of the psychology world. It has worked where many other forms of therapy have not. It is powerful! In fact, it is so powerful that many of the books written about it contain a chapter warning MI-ers not to unethically manipulate people with it.

If you are the type of person who loves research and wants to see the evidence for MI for yourself, I've included a list of research articles in the appendices.

Why Use MI? Because It Works *Quickly*!

The research support for MI is staggering. Lots of counseling styles work, though. So why MI? Because it doesn't just work - it works **quickly**!

A lot of counselors use Cognitive Behavioral Therapy (CBT) because it works. It has decades of research supporting its effectiveness, and it has helped many people. The problem with CBT (and just about every other form of therapy) for school counselors is how long it takes. According to the Mayo Clinic (Mayo Clinic Staff, 2016), clients should expect CBT to show results after 10-20 sessions of 50 minutes each. We might wish we had that kind of time to spend with individual students, but we just don't.

What's the average length of time you spend with students? When students make appointments to see me, they are booked for 15 minutes on my calendar. I wish I had more time with individual students, but I'm just stretched too thin (*see previous rant about caseloads*). Fifteen minutes isn't much time to have a meaningful impact on students...***unless*** you're using MI!

Motivational Interviewing can absolutely be used for 15 minutes with life-altering results. In fact, the average amount of time MI is used in research projects is 1 to 4 sessions for 15 minutes each (Miller & Rollnick, 2013). In other words, the mountain of research showing that MI is effective is based mainly on studies in which MI is used for the same amount of time we school counselors have with our students. If you've read much research (no judgment if you haven't - most of it is booooring), you know how unusual this is. Most research projects investigating the effectiveness of other forms of therapy base their findings on 3 to 5 sessions of 50 minutes each.

What does all this mean? MI is ***potent*** - far more potent than other forms of therapy. School counselors need something that works quickly, and MI is it!

Goal for the Week

This week, do something to celebrate yourself and the thousands of ways you've changed students' lives. Be good to yourself! Thank you for what you do, and thank you for wanting to be even better at it!

(In future chapters, I will give you specific goals to shoot for as you learn to use MI.)

PART I:

EMPATHY

Empathy Is a Skill, Not a Feeling

Part I of this book is about the skill of showing empathy. MI can't be done well without empathy. In fact, being an impactful school counselor is impossible without being a world-class show-er of empathy. One of the great things about MI is that it has sharpened some time-tested client-centered techniques devoted to showing empathy so they are even more effective. The first part of this book is a crash course in using these potent skills.

CHAPTER 1:

Simple Reflections & Open-Ended Questions

The following chapter presents skills that may seem simple to some and difficult to others based on their current counseling style. Hopefully, almost everyone will hear echoes of things they learned in their graduate programs. As I've talked with counselors from across the country, I've found that many feel being thrown around by the tornadoes of their everyday duties have caused them to lose sight of basic skills. I always start MI trainings with a refresher of the essential building blocks for empathic relationships with students. MI simply cannot be done without them. Actually, no form of therapy can. Research is clear that the most powerful predictor of good outcomes is counselors' ability to show empathy (Lambert & Barley, 2001; Elliott, Bohart, Watson & Greenberg, 2011; Horvath & Symonds, 1991). If in reading this chapter you long for more complex skills, fear not! The more advanced maneuvers are a mere few pages away.

The Skill (not feeling) of Empathy

Empathy is like any other skill - it doesn't matter how you *feel*; it matters what you *do*. I can feel like a professional football player all day long, but until I tackle a 220-lb. receiver who runs like an Olympic sprinter (unlikely considering my 5' 9" frame and geriatric-level speed), I'm not one. The same is true for people in helping professions who deeply care about their clients but don't know how to show it very well.

There is a dangerous delusion threatening school counselors here. We got into this profession because we care about students and want to see them live their lives to the fullest. We *cannot* assume, though, that our students believe this to be true. They don't know our hearts. They don't know how deeply we do or do not care about them. All they know is what we *do.* If we want our students to know how much we care, we had better nail the *skill* of empathy.

If you asked most people (school counselors included) for a definition of empathy, they'd probably say something like, "understanding another person's perspective." The problem is, according to this definition, we can't know people are empathic - only they know because only they really know what they understand. MI takes empathy further. It isn't just about how well you understand people's perspective; it's how well you *show* them that you understand. Here's an MI definition of empathy for school counselors:

Empathy: the ability to understand students' perspectives *AND* to accurately reflect their perspectives back to them.

There is a ton of research investigating what skills counselors can use to show empathy to clients. This is like gold for school counselors! Unfortunately, many of us don't learn these skills in our graduate programs or in day-to-day work. Learning to use MI starts with being world-class at showing empathy, so we will focus the next few chapters on exactly that.

Reflective Listening

According to research (Moyers & Miller, 2013; Miller, Benefield, & Tonigan, 1993; Miller, Taylor, & West, 1980; Miller & Baca, 1983; Patterson & Forgatch, 1985) the key to showing empathy is **reflective listening**, or responding to students more often with statements than with questions. For example...

> **Student:** "I can't stand that class!"

> **Counselor:** "You really don't enjoy being in that class."

As opposed to...

> **Student:** "I can't stand that class!"

> **Counselor:** "Why do you hate it so much?"

At first, this seems counter-intuitive. Doesn't asking a question mean you're asking for more information so you can understand the student better? Sure, it does. But think of it this way - if you have to ask the student why he/she hates the class, doesn't that inherently mean you *don't* understand why they hate it? And doesn't that mean you really *don't* empathize with them yet? Remember that empathy is an action, not a feeling. You care about the student regardless of whether you ask a question or make a statement, but making a reflective statement makes the student feel more understood.

When I first learned about reflective listening in grad school, I thought it sounded completely crazy. Why would I repeat back to students what they're saying? Won't they say, *"Duh! That's what I just said!"* It took me a while of making myself reflect students' statements before I believed it wouldn't blow up in my face. For the record, I've never had a student respond in that way, and there are good reasons why.

First, reflective listening makes students feel like you *get* them. In the above example, when the counselor says, "You really don't enjoy being in that class," the student's likely response is something like, "Exactly, because..." He/she would feel that the counselor understands where he/she is coming from and will want to say more as a result. Adolescents desperately want to be understood, but they rarely feel as thought adults empathize with them. When they do, they jump at the opportunity to be known.

Secondly, reflective listening keeps the spotlight of the conversation on the student. In this analogy, an interaction between a counselor and a student is a scene in a play with the student and counselor being actors. In our offices, we want students to be the stars! What goes on in our offices should be all about students. Consider what happens in the above interaction. If the counselor simply reflects what the student says, the focus (aka, the spotlight) is placed firmly on the student and his/her thoughts. However, if the counselor asks a question, the spotlight shifts to him/her because what happens next is a product of the counselor's question (not the student's statement). In other words, the counselor has taken control of the conversation because what happens next is dependent on the question he/she chooses to ask, *not* the statement the student already made. Consider another example:

> **Student:** "Last night, my parents told me they're getting a divorce."

If the counselor asks a question, the conversation will go in the direction the counselor chooses.

> **Counselor:** "Did they explain why?"

or

> "When are they going to separate?"

or

> "How surprised were you?"

However, if the counselor simply reflects the student's statement, the student will then have the freedom to take the conversation toward whatever is most pressing on his/her heart.

> **Counselor:** "Your parents are ending their marriage."

At this point, the student can decide where to go from here.

Student: "They said they don't want to fight anymore."

or

"Yes, and they said dad is moving out this weekend."

or

"Ya, and it's scary because..."

We more clearly show empathy when we give students the spotlight. More often than not, they will steer the conversation where it needs to go. When we ask questions, we're taking the wheel, but we don't know as well as they do where we should go.

Third, reflective listening gives students the space to *process*. Here's a little-known but profound fact: **Most people process AFTER they speak.** Most of the time, your students haven't plumbed the depths of their hearts and uncovered the truths that drive their thoughts, actions, and feelings. They are simply stating what is on the front of their minds in the moment. They need help really thinking through what they're saying, and reflective listening gives them the space to process.

Student: "That teacher hates me."

Counselor: "Your teacher doesn't like you on a personal level."

> **Student:** "I don't know. Maybe not. She just tells me to be quiet a lot."

In this example, the student hasn't considered that, when he says his teacher hates him, he's really saying his teacher has a personal issue with him. By reflecting, the counselor gives him a chance to come to this realization and back off the statement. It doesn't seem like much, but a realization like this could change the student's relationship with this teacher!

Simple Reflections

Without further delay, let's learn how to do some reflective listening! There are 2 kinds of reflective listening: **simple reflections** and **complex reflections**. We'll stick with the, um, simpler of the two in this chapter and move on to the more, well, complex in the next chapter. A **simple reflection** is repeating a few words or ideas back to the student so they can delve a little deeper into what they're thinking about. Here's an example from a conversation I had with a student today...

> **Student:** "Boys are so annoying!"

> **Counselor:** *[raises his eyebrow]*

> **Student:** "Not you. I mean teenage boys. I told this guy I wasn't interested in him, but he keeps talking to me. I can't believe it!"

Counselor: "You told him you don't want to date him, but he doesn't get it." ***Simple Reflection***

Student: "Right! We FaceTime-ed until 11 last night, and I told him I just want to be friends. It's frustrating!"

By reflecting the main idea my student shared (she told the guy she wasn't interested, but he kept pursuing her), I gave her the opportunity to share that she was frustrated. This is a step in the right direction in her processing her situation, *and* she feels that I empathize with her.

Simple reflecting is essentially parroting a few choice words or ideas that students share. What you choose to reflect will play a large role in where the conversation goes, so choose wisely. In the above example, I could have chosen to reflect another part of her conversation, but it wouldn't have led anywhere useful.

Student: "Boys are so annoying!"

Counselor: *[raises his eyebrow]*

Student: "Not you. I mean teenage boys. I told this guy I wasn't interested in him, but he keeps talking to me. I can't believe it!"

Counselor: "You think teenage boys are more annoying than adult men." ***Simple Reflection***

> **Students:** "Well, ya. Adults aren't annoying, I guess. Because they're older."

You can see that, if I had chosen to reflect the wrong part of her statement, the conversation wouldn't have gone anywhere constructive or really been helpful to her. Be sure to reflect the main point of the student's statement.

If you're reflecting well, you'll rarely have to ask questions. Most students will continue to share what they're thinking with greater depth as you reflect their thoughts back to them. In fact, according to typical MI standards, a good MI session includes at least twice as many reflections as questions. Continuing with the previous example...

> **Student:** "Right! We FaceTime-ed until 11 last night, and I told him I just want to be friends. It's frustrating!"
>
> **Counselor:** You talked to him a ton last night, and it ended in your being frustrated."
>
> **Student:** "Ya! I don't know what I have to do to get him to understand. I just want to be friends."
>
> **Counselor:** "You don't know what you could do to make him get it."
>
> **Student:** "Ya, we talked for hours last night. At the end, it seemed like he didn't get it any more than at the beginning."

Counselor: "All that talking didn't do a thing."

Student: "No! Maybe I need to talk to him less. I want to still be friends, but it seems like talking just makes him think I like him."

The great thing about this interaction is that the *student* came to the realization that she might want to do something different next time. As a counselor with a bunch of experience with teenage boys, I could have told her at the beginning of the conversation that talking to a boy until 11pm doesn't tell him to back off, no matter how many times she said it. However, if I had interrupted her learning process at that point, two things would likely have happened: 1) she would *not* feel cared for by me, and 2) she probably wouldn't have been changed at all. Why is this?

A *very* important principle in MI is that **people listen to themselves**. The concept makes logical sense when you think about it, especially in the context of adolescents. The *last* thing a typical teenager wants is for adults to tell him/her what to believe or how to live. It's plenty true for adults, too - we're just more skilled at pretending it's not true. The beauty of reflective listening is that the student is working out the problem with your help. You're not telling him/her what to do. If you did, he/she likely wouldn't listen anyway.

If you're not used to doing a lot of reflecting, it can be quite a mind-bender at first. Simple reflections are nice because you can use students' own words. You don't have to come up with the words; your goal is to pick the right words to reflect so that the conversation goes in the most constructive direction. As you get comfortable with simple reflections, you can move on to more complex reflections (see Chapter 2).

Reflection Pointers

The Art of the Pause. Once you have used a simple reflection, you have to **PAUSE**. It's tempting to quickly follow up a reflection with a question when students don't respond right away. *Do not* do this. It sucks the life right out of your reflection. If uncomfortable silence gets on your nerves, it's time to get over it.

> **Student:** "I hate this school."

> **Counselor:** "You hate this school."

> (PAUSE!)

It would be *so* easy at this point to ask, "What do you hate about our school?" Resist! If you sit quietly, the vast majority of students will fill the silence. They'll tell you exactly what you want to know *and* they'll feel like you get them. Remember, this is all about *empathy*. Students feel far more understood when you're reflecting as opposed to asking questions.

Don't Turn Reflections into Questions. It's common when you first commit to doing more reflections to turn them into questions by using an upward inflection at the end of your statement. This is how we ask questions in the English language. It's not how we make reflective statements. If you're going to inflect upwards, you may as well ask a question. This is another common temptation that is difficult to fight at first. Stay strong. Reject the inflect!

Don't Say, "What I Hear...". In the not-so-distant past, those entering the counseling profession were trained to say things like, "What I'm hearing is..." or "What I hear you saying is..." before they made a reflective statement. Don't do this. *Of course* the next thing you say is what you're hearing. You don't need to say so. It just makes you sound like a therapist. Avoid that stereotype like the plague! There aren't a lot of adolescents lining up to see therapists.

Instead of using one of these therapeutic-sounds phrases, either use no introductory phrase at all or use "It sounds like..."

> **Student:** "Spanish class is *sooooooo* boring."

> **Counselor:** "You really don't like sitting through your Spanish class."

> *or*

> "It sounds like Spanish class is a real drag for you."

Open-Ended Questions

Questions aren't the devil. They're just not as powerful as reflections. It's not bad to ask questions occasionally as long as they're the right kind. What's that kind? Open-ended questions.

Open-Ended Questions are questions that cannot be answered with "yes" or "no," whereas closed-ended questions are yes/no questions.

> **Counselor:** "How are things going in your classes?" *Open-Ended Question*

> **Counselor:** "Do you know you're failing 2 classes?" *Closed-Ended Question*

Closed-ended questions generally make a person feel less understood because the spotlight of the conversation is firmly on the counselor. The counselor is doing all the processing and is throwing out ideas for the student to affirm or deny.

> **Counselor:** "Do you think you're struggling because you're not doing all of the homework?" *Closed-Ended Question*

> **Student:** "I guess so."

> **Counselor:** "Do you have a quiet place to do assignments at home?" *Closed-Ended Question*

> **Student:** "No, not really."

Counselor: "Do you think you should talk to your mom about creating one for you?" ***Closed-Ended Question***

Student: "Ok."

In this scenario, the counselor is diagnosing the problem and coming up with his/her perceived solution while the student watches. There are lots of problems with this: 1) the student isn't processing anything, which means he/she isn't coming to a greater understanding of the situation, 2) the counselor is assuming he/she knows the problem without getting any significant information from the student, and 3) the student doesn't feel a speck of empathy.

Open-ended questions are better because they let students do the work. They know what's going on in their lives and in their hearts. As much experience as we have with students, we can't know for sure what is the most pressing issue rolling around in students' souls. Open-ended questions give them the space to explore that themselves.

Counselor: "What do you think is causing you to struggle in your classes?" ***Open-Ended Question***

Student: "Well, I'm not doing a lot of homework. That's bringing down my grades."

Counselor: "What's holding you back from doing homework?" ***Open-Ended Question***

> **Student:** "I have to watch my little sister when I get home from school because my mom works late. So, I don't have much time to do it."

When the counselor used closed-ended questions, the solution to the perceived problem came completely from the counselor and wasn't really a solution to what was going on. Asking the same student open-ended questions led to the true problem, not what the counselor assumed was the problem.

Open-Ended Questions Are...Ok

Open-ended questions are way better than closed-ended questions, but they don't lead to students experiencing empathy like reflections do. Said another way, open-ended questions are an open door to empathy because the counselor can reflect students' answers to open-ended questions. Closed-ended questions slam the door on empathy. You can't reflect "yes" or "no." If you can use a reflection, do it. If all that will fit the conversation is a question, use an open-ended one and then reflect the answer.

Most school counselors I've talked with were trained to use open-ended questions and rely on them far more than reflections. Certainly this is better than lecturing students or asking closed-ended questions, but there's a danger to it as well. Too many open-ended questions can easily feel like an interrogation.

Counselor: "What do you think is causing your grades to suffer?" *Open-Ended Question*

Student: "It's probably that I don't do all the homework."

Counselor: "What's holding you back from doing your homework?" *Open-Ended Question*

Student: "My mom works late, so I have to take care of my little sister."

Counselor: "When do you pick up your little sister from school?" *Open-Ended Question*

Student: "3:30."

Counselor: "And when do you feed her dinner?" *Open-Ended Question*

Student: "Usually around 6."

Counselor: "How much time do you have at nights to do homework?" *Open-Ended Question*

At best, a string of open-ended questions like this feels nothing like empathy and, at worst, feels like a cross-examination during a criminal trial. Beware of using too many open-ended questions! The best way to avoid it is to always reflect students' answers after asking an open-ended question.

The bottom line is that open-ended questions are neutral. They can be a conduit to reflective listening, and that's a good thing! Just don't rely on them.

Remember...The Goal is Empathy

It can be easy to get caught up in "this technique is better than that one" and "that one is better than this one." Remember that the goal here is to show **empathy**. We are working with adolescents who feel, at best, misunderstood and, at worst, abandoned by the adult world. Learning to *show* them empathy can change their lives because it helps them trust the adults around them who are trying to help. We got into this field because we care about students. Reflective listening is how we *show* them that.

Goal For the Week

Use 3 simple reflections during each student appointment this week.

Extra Credit: Who doesn't love extra credit! Practice on your friends, significant others, kids, etc. The more you reflect, the more normal it feels (and the more you show empathy to those around you).

BONUS MATERIAL 1:

How to Be a *Terrible* School Counselor!

Sometimes, when you're learning new skills, it helps to know what *not* to do. Here are a few things you don't want to do. Ever.

1. Give Lots of Advice

This is a common mistake. We all fall prey to this one at times. According to MI, there's a good reason. It's *called* **The Righting Reflex.**

The Righting Reflex is the inherent desire in most counselor-type folks to fix what is wrong with our students and set them on the right course. We care, after all! We want them to live the best lives they can possibly live, and we're pretty confident we know exactly what they need to do. How could we not tell them?

> **Counselor:** "You *have* to stop smoking weed. Do you know that it stunts the development of your brain? Here's what I think we need to do - let's get you connected with our substance abuse specialist. I really care about you, so I want you to get help."

The reason The Righting Reflex is *wrong* is because students aren't moved by our advice, even if it's the best advice of all time. Remember this central MI principle: your students are *much* more likely to do what they say, not what you or other people say. Don't take it personally. It doesn't mean they don't love you or appreciate your advice. It's just the way we humans are. We all listen to ourselves.

This is particularly true of adolescents. They are striving for autonomy from adults, which means they are even *more* likely to listen to themselves. When we give advice, most students will politely listen to your opinion and even agree that it's correct. Some will even say they will follow your advice, but they probably won't. How many times have you checked in on a student to find that he/she didn't follow through on the plan you had created for them? A hundred? A thousand? Me too. Oftentimes, that's because it was your plan, not the student's plan.

Rejecting the temptation to give advice is one of the hardest parts of MI. It takes some time to get used to, but it's *so* worth it. What's the antidote to The Righting Reflex? **Reflective Listening**. If you're reflecting what students are saying, you can't be responding to your own need to fix their situation.

> **Counselor:** "No judgment here. I'm just asking because I care about you. What do you think about your marijuana use?" ***Open-Ended Question***

Student: "I don't think it's a big deal. Maybe I should smoke a little less during the week, though."

Counselor: "You don't think it's a huge problem, but you're thinking about cutting back during the week." ***Simple Reflection***

2. Bring Your Own Agenda

Oftentimes, when we are calling students into our offices, it's because they are failing a number of classes, another staff member has referred them because they experienced intense emotions in class, they are getting into trouble on a regular basis, etc. That means we have an implied agenda for the meeting - help students raise their grades, deal with emotions, regulate their behavior, and so on.

The problem with letting our agenda drive interactions with students is that *all* humans (not just teens) feel negative emotions when they perceive their freedom is being threatened. It's called psychological reactance for the psychology nerds like me in the audience. Adolescents feel this particularly strongly because autonomy is a major characteristic of their developmental stage. They don't want adults telling them what they should do or how they should feel. Psychological reactance can look different with different students.

Verbal Rebellion

> **Counselor:** "I called you down because your math teacher said you weren't doing much work in her class."

> **Student:** "I don't really care what she thinks."

Closing Off Relationship

> **Counselor:** "I called you down because your math teacher said you weren't doing much work in her class."

> **Student:** "Ok."

Happily Lying to Your Face

> **Counselor:** "I called you down because your math teacher said you weren't doing much work in her class."

> **Student:** "Oh ya! I was planning on going in today after school to get extra help. I really want to get my grade up in there."

Usually, the only students who will verbally rebel have experienced trauma in their past and are always ready for a fight with adults. Most teens are more subtle with the tactics they employ to avoid your agenda. They will either be as tight-lipped as possible until they can get out of your office (closing off relationship), or they will tell you exactly what you want to hear with no intention of following through (happily lying to your face). The last response is the most dangerous because it makes you and other adults think you're changing students' lives for the better when you're not. It's a favorite tactic among socially aware teens because it works so well! All the adults around them are happy for months or even years until they finally catch on that the students never intended to follow adults' agendas even though they verbally agreed to them. This has happened to *all* of us.

The problem with bringing your own agenda is that students do what *they* say they are going to do, not what you say they should do. Again, people listen to themselves. Thankfully, this does *not* mean counselors can't bring their own ideas to the table when using MI. There's just a particular way to do it. We'll get into it in detail in a future chapter, but here's an appetizer.

> **Counselor:** "I called you down because I have something I'd like to talk about, but I want to know what is on your mind first. How have you been? How's life?"

3. Be One More Typical Adult in Students' Lives

Consider what teenagers experience from most adults in their lives, particularly those connected to their school experience. Teachers want them to perform academically. Administrators want them to conform to the school rules.

Coaches want them to practice with full intensity and play to the height of their ability. Parents want all of the above.

How do these adults try to get adolescents to do what they're supposed to do? With *external* force.

> **Teacher:** "If you don't turn in your project, I'll have to give you an F for the quarter."

> **Admin:** "I'm going to have to give you detention for your dress code violation."

> **Coach:** "If you forget the play one more time, I'm sitting you."

> **Parent:** "*Please*, just do what I know you're capable of."

The problem with external force is that it doesn't lead to lasting change. With some students, it will work for a while. The problem is that the change is flimsy - it disappears as soon as the external threat subsides.

Long-lasting change requires an internal process (Naar-King & Suarez, 2011). By using MI principles, you can invite students to experience an internal process of change. You can be different than the other adults in their lives. Here's something I say to students almost every day:

Counselor: "For a minute, forget all the adults in your life - your parents, your teachers, me - what do *you* want for yourself academically? What would success look like for *you*?" ***Open-Ended Question***

Student: "I'd be happy with A's and B's. I can definitely do that."

Counselor: "Getting all A's and B's is something that matters to you." ***Complex Reflection (spoiler alert!)***

Again, *reflective listening* is the antidote. If you're reflecting what students are saying, you're *not* acting like the other adults in their lives.

The Thought Life of a Counselor Learning Reflective Listening

As you probably noticed, the solution to being a terrible school counselor is reflective listening. If you're not used to doing a lot of reflecting, it is *hard* at first. You have to be thinking about what you're going to say before you say it while keeping the conversation going at a natural pace. There's no getting around the fact that learning to rely primarily on reflective listening is hard...which makes it like everything else worth doing! Things that have a significant impact in the world aren't easy. Take heart, though! Reflective listening gets easier quickly, especially as you begin to see the results that come with it - namely, students experiencing **empathy**.

So what's it like to be a counselor learning reflective listening? At first, your thought life is something like this:

> **Student:** "I'm so behind. I'll probably fail this class."

What counselor thinks about saying:

> **Counselor:** "No, you won't! You'll be fine!" *...wait, no. That's just my opinion.*

> **Counselor:** "Let's look at a way to keep track of your assignments." *...no, no. That's The Righting Reflex.*

> **Counselor:** "But don't you know how important graduating is??" *Definitely not. I sound like his mom.*

> **Counselor:** "Does it make you nervous that your grades are bad?" *Nope, Closed- Ended Question. I'm doing all the work.*

> **Counselor:** "You're so behind you're afraid you won't be able to get caught up." *YES! Reflective listening!*

Reflective listening takes a ton of mental effort at first, but it's so worth it. Your students are worth it! Once your go-to form of interacting with students is reflective listening, you'll be amazed at the relationships you build. Students will want to talk with you about making changes in their lives because they experience empathy in your office like nowhere else. Students' lives will change in front of your eyes!

CHAPTER 2:

Complex Reflections

Change Comes from (Deep) Within

As we talked about in the previous chapter, change that lasts only comes from within. Pressure from the outside won't do it, whether it's a parent cajoling or a counselor asking closed-ended questions. This concept is fine and dandy for Motivational Interviewers, as we believe people already have the potential within them to live life to the fullest. It's the calling of the school counselor to draw deeply held desires out of students so they can realize their potential.

How do we do this? You probably won't be surprised that a big part of the answer is *reflective listening*. As people share their hearts with us, we become a mirror reflecting it back to them so they can see what's in their souls and think about how to practically live it out. The reality for most of us in our hectic modern lives is that we don't get to think on a deep level very often. This is *especially* true for adolescents. How often are students asked to consider the deep things of life in school, whether it's in 4th grade or senior year? The reality for most adolescents is that they're living in an adult world with a bunch of grown-ups telling them what to do and think (even if they don't realize they're doing it). As we help students think on a soul-stirring level, we are helping them uncover what they believe about themselves and their world. At the same time, we are helping them unearth the *motivation* they need to live out what they believe. This is *life-changing* stuff!

Complex Reflections

Enter **Complex Reflections**. Complex reflections are, well, more complex than the simple reflections from the previous chapter. When counselors use complex reflections, they're not simply restating what clients have already said - they're appealing to what is *behind* clients' statements. What is in clients' hearts that compels them to say certain things? *That* is what we really want to appeal to, because that is the driving force of lasting change.

The creators of Motivational Interviewing use an iceberg metaphor to describe the difference between simple and complex reflections (Miller & Rollnick, 2013). Somewhere around 90% of an iceberg lies below the surface of the frigid water it inhabits. In the same way, much of what motivates our actions lies beneath the surface. Simple reflections are limited to what students have overtly shared regarding what drives their decisions, whereas complex reflections explore the 90% that is unexpressed.

At this point, some of you might be thinking, *How do I know what motivates students on a deep level?* Good question! The truth is that we'll never be able to identify everything that motivates every student. The students on your caseloads are vastly different. They all have unique genetic blueprints and experiences. However, there are some similar characteristics that drive the internal motivation of most people. Simply stated, they are **Emotions**, **Goals**, and **Values**. Complex reflections "make guesses" about what feelings, goals, and values are motivating students in a particular situation (Miller & Rollnick, 2013, p. 57).

Emotions

> **Student:** "My sister doesn't want me to smoke so much."
>
> **Counselor:** "You're thinking about cutting back because you love your sister." *Complex Reflection of Emotion*

Emotions are a gold mine when building relationships with adolescents. Most of them are experiencing a wide range of emotions every day, more so in adolescence than in any other season of life. Most of them don't hide that fact if counselors just scratch the surface a little. I had this conversation with a student today:

> **Counselor:** "I just wanted to check in with you because I heard through the grapevine that something sad happened with your family."
>
> **Student:** "Ya, but I'm fine. It's ok."
>
> **Counselor:** "Ok. I hear you telling me that you're fine, but your tone of voice makes it sound like you're feeling pretty sad." *Complex Reflection of Emotion*

Student: *[tearing up]* "Ya, it has been hard today. I've just been trying to be ok."

Not only do most adolescents experience a significant number of emotions every day, but they are also open to talking about them. Although many of them give the impression they don't want to talk about their feelings, it's usually a generic defense mechanism they have learned to use against all adults because they aren't used to adults being empathic with them. Once you use Reflective Listening to show you empathize with them, the emotions will flow. And your relationship with them will grow. And the seeds of change will be planted! Here's a conversation I had this week:

Student: "Ya, I cheated on those tests. I just don't know what to do to get a good grade in that class."

Counselor: "You're worried because you're not sure how to do well in the class, yet cheating only got you a zero on a couple of tests."
Complex Reflection of Emotion

Student: "Ya, it didn't even work. And it sucks because I've worked so hard in that class."

Counselor: "It's gotta be frustrating to work really hard in the class and not see results."
Complex Reflection of Emotion

Student: "Yes, and now my parents are ticked at me, too."

Counselor: "You're anxious about disappointing your parents." ***Complex Reflection of Emotion***

In the span of a few sentences, this student shared three different emotions with me. It was a powerful opportunity to show empathy, as I got three chances to show her that I understood how she felt and that I cared.

Unfortunately, some counselors steer clear of reflecting emotions because of their own fear of addressing peoples' feelings (Resnicow, 2008). Adolescents are emotional beings, and they don't have a ton of life experience to help them process how they feel. Unresolved, intense emotions (whether they be positive, negative, or somewhere in between) can cause adolescents to make all kinds of unusual decisions. In fact, some MI experts believe that students get stuck in ambivalence toward positive life changes because they don't want to experience uncomfortable emotions (Naar-King & Suarez, 2011). Helping students process their emotions by simply reflecting their feelings can be life-changing for them. Let's not shrink back from the opportunity! Here's one more example from a conversation I had with a student this week:

Student: "Some bad stuff happened in my family when I was a kid."

Counselor: "It hurt you pretty badly." ***Complex Reflection of Emotion***

Student: "Ya, but it was a long time ago."

Counselor: "Yet you still feel the pain from it." ***Complex Reflection of Emotion***

Student: *[tearing up]* "Ya, I think it affects me a lot."

Counselor: "It makes you nervous to think about how that stuff in the past affects your life now." ***Complex Reflection of Emotion***

By reflecting my student's emotions, I gave her space to realize to a greater degree how much her painful past was influencing her present. The end result of the conversation was that the student, who had previously been reticent to seek mental health counseling, asked to meet again to discuss what seeing a therapist would be like.

At first, reflecting emotions can be an intimidating proposition. It can feel like juggling grenades. When you're learning to reflect emotions, use the simple phrase, "You're feeling..." Once you use this for a few days, you'll likely feel comfortable mixing it up and using other ways to reflect feelings.

Goals

Student: "Someday, I want to have a big house so all my kids can have their own room."

> **Counselor:** "It's a goal of yours to take care of your family financially." ***Complex Reflection of Goal***

In addition to emotions, another deep motivating factor for our students (and all humans, for that matter) is their **goals**. This makes practical sense - we all make decisions in an effort to get us where we want to go. Many adolescents, whether they're 11 or 18, haven't thought much about why they do what they do. Said another way, their actions are moving them along a particular path, but they haven't really thought about where that path leads. That's where we come in!

> **Student:** "I hate moving between my mom's place and my dad's place every week."

> **Counselor:** "You don't want your kids to experience that in the future." ***Complex Reflection of Goal***

> **Student:** "Heck no! I'll do whatever it takes to not get divorced."

There are a couple of things to note in this example. First, remember that the main goal of using complex reflections is to show students *empathy*. The student feels that the counselor understands what he/she wants in the future. Second, notice the educated guess the counselor is making. The student never said he/she doesn't want their kids to experience joint custody. That was a guess on the counselor's part. That's exactly what makes this a complex reflection. Here's another example from a conversation I had recently:

>**Student:** "I know I'm socially awkward. I bother some people."
>
>**Counselor:** "You really want to make some friends here." *Complex Reflection of Goal*
>
>**Student:** "Ya, I want to have some people I can talk to who aren't adults."

The timeline for goals is generally insignificant. It doesn't matter if it's a goal for the afternoon or for the next 30 years. The important thing is that the goal is motivating. With high school students, it's helpful to ask them what they're hoping to accomplish a long way down the road. As their counselors, we're trying to help them think about their post-high school plans anyway.

>**Counselor:** "When you're 80 years old, how will you know if you've lived a life worth living?"
>
>**Student:** "Hmm...I definitely want to have a big family. And I want to live in a big house in the country with a lot of land so my kids will have lots of space to play."
>
>**Counselor:** "A goal of yours is to have some wide open spaces for your family." *Complex Reflection of Goal*

With 4th graders, it's generally more appropriate to discuss their goals for the rest of the week or even the rest of the day because long-term goals will likely be less motivating to them. Regardless, if you're doing a good job of reflecting students, they will experience empathy and will usually pursue a deeper relationship with you.

> **Student:** "My mom said I can't spend the night with my friend on Friday if I have any more tardies this week."

> **Counselor:** "So the big goal for you in the next 2 days is to make it to every class on time." ***Complex Reflection of Goal***

As you're learning to reflect goals, the easiest way to get the hang of it is to use the introductory phrase, "A goal of yours is..." That way, you *know* you're reflecting a goal.

Values

> **Student:** "I thought we were best friends, but then she went behind my back and told people everything about me."

> **Counselor:** "That hurt pretty bad." ***Complex Reflection of Emotion***

> **Student:** "Ya, it sucked. I just don't think people should do that to each other."

Counselor: "Loyalty is really important to you." *Complex Reflection of Value*

Student: "Especially with best friends. If I can't trust her, who can I trust?"

Another door into students' hearts is their **values**. Unlike goals, values have an inherent moral stance. For example, students may value honesty, friendship, or success. They believe these are good things. Of course, these tend to lead to goals, but they're not the same thing as goals. Generally speaking, they're the motivation beneath the goal. That's why reflecting values is usually more powerful than reflecting goals.

Student: "I need to get my grades up because my parents want me to go to a good college."

Counselor: "Your family is really important to you." *Complex Reflection of Value*

Student: "Ya, they've worked really hard to give me this opportunity. And I want to be able to take care of my parents when they're older."

Counselor: "It's important to you to be able to take care of your parents like they've taken care of you." *Complex Reflection of Value*

In the same way that values build the foundation for most goals, they are also the source of many emotions. Students feel strong positive emotions when things align with their values and strong negative ones when they do not.

> **Student:** *[crying]* "How could she say that about me online?"

> **Counselor:** "It's wrong to treat people like that."
> ***Complex Reflection of Value***

> **Student:** "Ya, it's just evil."

Remember that the ultimate goal is empathy. If students think you get their deep-seated values, how could they not feel understood?

As you're learning to reflect values, you can simply say, "You value..." My favorite way to reflect values, though, is to say, "It's important to you that..." Value isn't a word we use often in our culture outside of a good sale at the mall, so saying something is important usually makes more sense to students.

"But What If I Guess Wrong?"

When we're reflecting something that hasn't overtly been stated (i.e., using a complex reflection), by definition, we have to make some guesses. What if we guess wrong? This is a common fear of counselors who are just getting accustomed to using complex reflections. Here's the good news - it almost never matters! The reason is because students will typically just correct you.

> **Student:** "Mrs. Ross makes me *so* angry!"
>
> **Counselor:** "You get so angry in her class, you could throw a desk across the room!" ***Complex Reflection of Emotion***
>
> **Student:** "Well, maybe not *that* angry. But sometimes I at least want to throw a pencil!"

The great thing about guessing wrong is that students *still* feel understood when they correct you. In my experience, there's little (if any) difference in how much students experience empathy between a perfect guess and a missed guess. Either way, they know the counselor is trying to understand them, and they get the chance to explain how they feel, what they think, etc. Oftentimes, students themselves don't know exactly how they feel *until* they correct the counselor. They're discovering their emotions/goals/values as they speak.

Choosing What to Reflect

Students provide a ton of information within the span of a few minutes. As we choose what to reflect, we're likely deciding in what direction the conversation will go. We need to choose wisely!

> **Student:** "I really like sleeping in, but last Saturday, my mom woke me up early to tell me

she needed to take my little sister to the hospital."

Counselor: "That must have been scary!" ***Complex Reflection of Emotion***

or

"Sleeping in is important to you." ***Complex Reflection of Value***

Both of these are complex reflections, but it's pretty clear that the more empathic move here is to talk with the student about how it felt to be surprised by her little sister having to go to the hospital. What we choose to reflect influences the direction of our conversations, and our conversations influence the lives of our students. We need to be strategic. Here's another example:

Student: "I want to cut back on how much weed I've been smoking. My dad is a total alcoholic, and it's annoying."

Counselor: "You don't want to be an addict like your dad." ***Complex Reflection of Goal***

or

"Your dad frustrates you." ***Complex Reflection of Emotion***

Either of reflections would be effective in making the student feel heard. The question for the counselor is: where do you want the conversation to go? The first reflection will likely lead the student to talk about using less, while the second will likely lead the student to talk more about his/her father. Be sure to match your reflection to your goal for the conversation.

Complex Reflections vs. Open-Ended Questions

As mentioned in the previous chapter, reflections (especially complex ones) lead to students feeling understood whereas open-ended questions do not. Questions aren't evil, though. There are plenty of times when you'll ask questions in a conversation. When you do, *make sure* you follow the student's response with a reflection.

> **Counselor:** "How's your stress level on a scale of 1 to 10?" ***Open-ended Question***
>
> **Student:** "I'd say about a 7."
>
> **Counselor:** "Your stress is all the way up to a 7." ***Simple Reflection***
>
> **Student:** "Ya. I just can't get my Algebra grade up to where I want it."
>
> **Counselor:** "It's important to you to succeed academically." ***Complex Reflection of Value***

On a commonly-used scale to assess the effectiveness of a MI session, counselors who have a 2:1 ratio of reflections to open-ended questions are considered competent (The scale is called the Motivational Interviewing Treatment Integrity scale - Moyers, Rowell, Manuel, Ernst, & Houck, 2016). Counselors who have a ratio of 3:1 or more are considered to be advanced in their MI skill.

As you're starting out on the journey to being a MI-skilled counselor, the best way to ensure that your ratio of reflections to questions is at least 2:1 is to think of the pattern **Reflect - Ask - Reflect**. *Reflect* a student, then *ask* a question, and finally *reflect* their answer.

> **Student:** "I'm thinking about smoking less during basketball season."
>
> **Counselor:** "You want to play well this year, and smoking less will be part of that." ***Complex Reflection of Goal***
>
> **Student:** "Ya. I want to be able to play faster this year."
>
> **Counselor:** "How much do you want to cut back?" ***Open-Ended Question***
>
> **Student:** "I think I just want to smoke on the weekends. It's going to be hard though."
>
> **Counselor:** "You're nervous about how hard it will be." ***Complex Reflection of Emotion***

Goal for the Week

Try to use each kind of complex reflection at least once a day. To make it easier, write these phrases on a cheat sheet and stick it on your desk.

"You're feeling..." *"A goal of yours is..."* *"It's important to you that..."*

CHAPTER 3:

Autonomy & Asking Permission

Reflective listening in its simple and complex forms is the empathy pot of gold. But we all know you need a leprechaun and a rainbow to make it to any decent pot of gold. In the same way (...or maybe not), validating students' **autonomy** over their own lives is the bedrock on which an empathic relationship is built.

We all like autonomy. We all want to feel as if we are in control of our lives. Adolescents, however, *love* autonomy. It's one of the driving goals of their developmental stage (Clark, 2011). Most adolescents, though, feel like they have to fight for control over their lives, as the adults who surround them (parents, teachers, administrators, coaches, the crotchety old man who lives next door) are fond of bossing them around. Many of those annoying adults actually have the teens' best interest in mind, but it doesn't feel like it to them.

The fact that adolescents are desperate for autonomy is fine and dandy to MI-skilled school counselors, as student autonomy is essential to MI done well. Remember that MI relies upon drawing motivation for change from *within* students. MI is all about autonomy.

The Controlling Adult Schema

Remember that first psychology class you took as an undergrad? If so, you may remember the word *schema*. Schemas are essentially scripts that people bring into certain situations (Bandura, 2002). For example, when the door-to-door magazine salesperson knocks on our door, we respond a certain way... and it's probably a very different way than how we respond when the Girl Scouts come peddling their bite-size morsels of heaven.

Students bring a certain schema into interactions with adults - the **Controlling Adult Schema**. They assume adults are going to try and tell them what to do. In turn, most students play their part. It can look different depending on the student, but it's generally agreement in word and rebellion in action (e.g., "Why, I've never thought of doing my homework every night. Yes, I will start doing that tonight!" ...and they don't). As the creators of Motivational Interviewing say, students decide "whether and how to pursue change; that choice cannot be taken away" (Miller & Rollnick, 2013, p. 124).

As school counselors, we have to fight against the controlling adult schema getting hung around our necks. We don't want students to interact with us the way they do with most adults. How do we prevent it? First, we show empathy by using (you guessed it!) reflective listening. Second, we can verbally assure students. In other words, we can simply tell them we don't play the same role as other adults in their lives. Below is a list of ways I communicate this to my students. It's not intended to be an exhaustive list, and you don't have to use them word-for-word. It's just to give you the gist of what we're trying to do. I call them **Give Away Power Phrases/Questions** because, in using them, we are giving authority of the conversation over to students. In other words, we are encouraging their autonomy!

Give Away Power Phrases/Questions

"It's totally up to you. It's your life. In the end, you get to decide."

"If it weren't up to your parents, your teachers, the principal, or me, and it was just up to you, what would you do?"

"I'm *your* counselor, not your teacher's counselor or your parent's counselor. Ultimately, I'm here to help you."

"I'm not going to tell you what to do or think. I'm here to help you decide what you want for *yourself.*"

"I'm not going tell anyone anything you say unless I'm worried for someone's safety. You can talk this through with me without worrying about it getting to anyone else."

Here's an example of giving away power to a student:

> **Counselor:** "Hey, come on in. Thanks for coming down to my office. I called you in because one of your teachers said she was concerned about you."

Student: *[looking concerned]* "Ok. What about?"

Counselor: "I think she's concerned that your grade isn't as high as it could be. Is it ok if we talk about that for a few minutes?" ***Asking Permission** (we'll get to this later in the chapter)*

Student: "Ya, sure."

Counselor: "Before we get into it, I just want you to know that I'm *your* counselor, not your teacher's. I'm not going to tell your teacher anything about our conversation. I'm just here to help you get the kind of grades *you* want."

"But They'll Choose to Be Stupid!"

At first, using one of the Give Away Power Phrases/Questions is scary for many school counselors because, as one counselor fearfully stated to me, "But they'll choose to be stupid!" Undoubtedly, we've all seen many adolescents make some poor decisions. As we talked about in the Introduction, adolescents routinely have higher rates of risky behavior, unprotected sex, and substance use than any other age group (Park, Mulye, Adams, Brindis, & Irwin, 2006). How can we trust them with autonomy?

The reality is that we have no choice. They are their own people who make their own decisions. They have autonomy whether the adults around them like it or not. As educators, it's our job to help them be prepared for adult life when they will be making decisions for themselves and their families.

One of the main goals of education is to propel students into autonomous adulthood.

Some of you might be thinking, *"Ya, but they're not ready for autonomy yet!"* Here's the good news: they're more ready than you might think. Remember that people have within them all they need to pursue healthy lives and, given the right environment, will naturally do exactly that. Don't believe me? Try a little experiment. Ask students what they want from themselves *apart* from adult expectations, and see what they say.

> **Counselor:** "It sounds like your parents have some pretty high expectations for you. Would it be ok if we put that aside and talk about what you want for a minute?" ***Asking Permission*** *(we'll get to this later in the chapter)*

> **Student:** "Sure."

> **Counselor:** "Ok, let's imagine for a minute that no adults care about what grades you make - your parents aren't pressuring you, your teachers aren't pressuring you, the administrators aren't pressuring you. What you make in classes is totally up to you. What would academic success look like? What would *you* be happy with?"

I have a conversation like this almost every day. In my experience, about 60% of students have about the same expectations for themselves as their parents. Another 30% of students actually have *higher* expectations of themselves. The last 10% have significantly lower expectations. I've found that many of the students in the last category have experienced some significant trauma in the past that causes them to have low expectations of themselves. In other words, the majority of students want the best for themselves and know that requires making good decisions. This is not limited to academics, either. I've had similar conversations about athletics, music, college applications, behavior in class, etc.

This begs the question - why do adolescents make bad decisions if they're internally motivated to live up to their potential? I can't say I have the definitive answer to that question, but I think one reason is *because* they're fighting for autonomy from adult control. Almost all humans are tempted to break certain rules simply because they are rules. If your significant other tells you not to look on the top shelf of a certain closet, what are the chances you will do exactly that in the next few days? Teenagers have the same inclination except that it's multiplied several times over because one of the goals of adolescence is autonomy (Clark 2011). My experience tells me that, if instead of proclaiming rules by adult decree, we acknowledge students' autonomy and help them process what they want for themselves, most students won't rebel. They'll thrive!

As you're considering how to provide students with opportunities to exercise their autonomy, their age and maturity level are certainly factors. Fourth graders making decisions about their lives look very different than 12th graders. Asking elementary schoolers what they want their lives to look like when they're 80 years old won't have as powerful an effect as asking high schoolers. There are some great ways to respect younger students' autonomy. One of the simplest ways is to simply ask them what they want to talk about. They're not used to adults letting them set the agenda for a meeting. This simple question blows their minds!

The School's Agenda

The idea of giving power of sessions over to students makes some counselors nervous, and for good reason: our duties are defined by the schools we serve. The district counseling director, school improvement plan, principal, department chair, and the American School Counselor Association all have priorities they expect us to pursue. How can we fulfill these expectations while also giving students autonomy in sessions?

Good news - MI allows for both! It does so in a beautifully simplistic way. In short, we can ask students what they want to talk about and also share what we want to discuss. Then, we let them decide what they want to talk about first.

> **Counselor:** "Hey, thanks for coming down to my office. Your Algebra teacher asked me to check in about how you're doing in her class. Before we get to that, though, what's new with you?"

> **Student:** "Well, since the last time we talked, my mom and I have been doing a lot better."

> **Counselor:** "That's great to hear! I want to hear more about that. What would you like to talk about first - Algebra class or your relationship with your mom?"

By clearly making our goal for the session known and also letting the student have input on the agenda, we are giving them autonomy while also getting to the topics we need to cover. To further give students power over the session, we also allow them to decide the order in which we cover the topics. It's so simple, yet it makes students feel respected. I've literally had students say, "Really?!" when I ask them to decide what we talk about first. Students aren't used to having control over their lives at school. It's blissfully surprising to them when we offer it to them.

Asking Permission

If our sharing the session agenda surprises students, asking permission *blows their minds!* **Asking permission** is exactly what it sounds like - counselors ask students if they are okay with talking about a particular topic.

> **Student:** "I had a good weekend. My friends and I went to a movie on Friday night. I worked on Saturday morning and did some homework in the afternoon. My whole family had a huge fight that night. It happens all the time. But then Sunday was cool. I went to the mall with a friend."

Counselor: "Overall, it was a good weekend for you. Something stood out to me - you said your family had a big fight and that it's a common thing." ***Simple Reflection***

Student: "Ya, at least once every weekend, everybody in the house ends up screaming at each other."

Counselor: "Would it be ok if we talk about that for a few minutes?" ***Asking Permission***

Student: "Sure."

You may have noticed that, in this example and the two previous examples of asking permission in the chapter, the question is closed-ended. Asking permission is one of the few times when it's fine to use a closed-ended question. We typically don't want to use closed-ended questions because they don't lead to students feeling empathy. In this case, however, they do! We are asking students for permission to do something. How could they *not* feel we respect them and want to know them!

Asking permission is especially powerful with students because adults in schools almost *never* ask them for permission to do anything. The same is true for adolescents in other areas of life. An adult deferring to them is a paradigm-shifting thing for them.

Remember that, as with everything else we've discussed in the last few chapters, the goal is empathy. How could students *not* feel that we care about them and that we want to know them when we are giving them control of sessions and asking permission? At the same time, we're reflecting their answers and helping them tap into the deep parts of their hearts. This is powerful stuff! Used well, these skills will help us build dynamic relationships with students.

Goal for the Week

Use a Give Away Power Phrase/Question or Ask for Permission at least once a day.

BONUS MATERIAL 2:

Empathy Checklist

As you're getting comfortable with using the skills in Part 1, have this checklist handy.

Simple Reflections

Reflect a few words or ideas shared by the student.

Complex Reflections

Emotions – *"You're feeling..."*

Goals – *"A goal of yours is..."*

Values – *"It's important to you that..."*

Autonomy & Asking Permission

Give Away Power Phrases/Questions

"It's totally up to you. It's your life. In the end, you get to decide."

"If it weren't up to your parents, your teachers, the principal, or me, and it was just up to you, what would you do?"

"I'm your counselor, not your teacher's counselor or your parent's counselor. Ultimately, I'm here to help you."

"I'm not going to tell you what to do or think. I'm here to help you decide what you want for yourself."

"I'm not going tell anyone anything you say unless I'm worried for someone's safety. You can talk this through with me without worrying about it getting to anyone else."

Asking Permission

"Would it be ok if..."

PART II:

CHANGE TALK

GROWING Change Talk, *shrinking* Sustain Talk

For the first part of this book, we've been learning ways that MI has tweaked client-centered techniques to build empathy-saturated relationships with students. In Part II, we're going to learn to use those empathic relationships to help students motivate themselves to change. MI is founded on the idea that people talk themselves into positive changes they want to make. For the rest of the book, we will be learning how to help our students do exactly that by GROWING Change Talk and *shrinking* Sustain Talk.

CHAPTER 4:

Change Talk vs. Sustain Talk

Motivational Interviewing doesn't work without empathy. We've spent several chapters making sure we don't just feel empathic but *show* empathy. If you don't feel comfortable with the skills we've learned so far and aren't seeing significant results from showing empathy, I'd suggest you return to Part I and work on your empathy skills. As mentioned earlier, research is quite clear that, with any counseling theory, the most powerful predictor of good outcomes is the counselor's relationship with the client (Lambert & Barley, 2001; Elliott, Bohart, Watson & Greenberg, 2011; Horvath & Symonds, 1991). There's no better way to build great relationships with students than by showing empathy. If you spent your whole career becoming a world-class show-er of empathy, you wouldn't be wasting your time.

For those who feel confident in their ability to show empathy, the next step of MI is **Change Talk**. You'll remember that MI, boiled down to its essential parts, can be defined as:

MI = Empathy + Change Talk

Change Talk and Sustain Talk

Stated simply, **Change Talk** consists of reasons, desires, abilities, needs, willingness, commitment, and steps toward change (Miller & Rollnick, 2013). As students are discussing a change they might want to make, we need to be listening very closely for Change Talk. Here are a few examples:

"If I got better grades, I know I'd have a better chance of going to college." ***Reason to Change***

"I want at least a 3.0 GPA." ***Desire to Change***

"I know I can do better in that class." ***Ability to Change***

"I need to make an A in math." ***Need to Change***

"I'd be willing to go to tutoring twice a week. ***Willingness to Change***

"I'm going to make a B in science." ***Commitment to Change***

"I studied before this week's quiz." ***Steps toward Change***

The type of Change Talk doesn't really matter. What matters is that we are able to notice Change Talk when it comes.

Sustain Talk, on the other hand, consists of reasons to keep things the way they are, to continue with the status quo. It can take all kinds of different forms, but here are a few examples:

> "I don't like studying."

> "School is boring."

> "My parents want me to go to _____ University, but I don't care."

> "That class is too hard."

> "I would go to tutoring after school, but that's the only time I have to hang out with my friends."

> "I'll start trying when I have to."

GROW Change Talk, *shrink* Sustain Talk

We've mentioned previously that, according to MI, students listen to themselves. As the creators of MI state, people "tend to become more committed to what they hear themselves saying" (Miller & Rollnick, 2013, p. 167). This being the case, if we can help students talk more about the positive change they're considering, they're more likely to actually make the change. In other words, we want to GROW the amount of Change Talk they're using.

At the same time, we want to shrink their amount of Sustain Talk. In the same way students can talk themselves into changing, they can also convince themselves to not change by discussing why they'd want to continue with the status quo.

Reflect Change Talk

How do we get students to use more Change Talk? Here's the great news: you don't have to learn any new skills! You simply reflect Change Talk when you hear it. In Part I, we discussed how reflecting students' statements makes them feel understood *and* encourages them to elaborate. When we reflect the Change Talk we hear students using, students feel more understood by us *and* they talk themselves into change.

> **Student:** "I want to meet some new people. It's just hard to do as a freshman." ***Change Talk and Sustain Talk***

> **Counselor:** "You're looking for some new friends." ***Simple Reflection***

> **Student:** "Ya. School would be a lot more fun if I knew more people."

In the same way that using Complex Reflections is the most potent way to show empathy, it is also the most impactful way to get students to delve into meaningful Change Talk. Again, no new skills! You're just using the skills you've worked hard to perfect. Continuing the previous example...

Counselor: "You want school to be more than just learning stuff. You want to enjoy life, and school is a big part of your life." *Complex Reflection of Goal*

Student: "Ya, it'd be boring otherwise." *Change Talk*

Counselor: "You don't just want to pass the time. You want to make memories with people." *Complex Reflection of Goal*

Student: "Ya, I want to do a bunch of fun things with different groups of people." *Change Talk*

Ask Questions about Change Talk

As with showing empathy, when it comes to GROWING Change Talk, it's better to use reflections. However, it is also perfectly appropriate to use some (not too many) open-ended questions to encourage students to talk more about change.

Student: "I think I want to start standing up for myself when that girl bullies me." *Change Talk*

Counselor: "What would that look like?" *Open-Ended Question*

Student: "I would stop being afraid of her and would tell her she's wrong." *Change Talk*

Note that this open-ended question helps the student delve deeper into the change. Making significant life changes is difficult. It's helpful to have considered what it would be like beforehand. As you're using open-ended questions, make sure the answer to your question will be Change Talk. We'll talk more about eliciting Change Talk with questions in the next chapter.

We mentioned in Chapter 1 that asking too many open-ended questions can make the conversation feel like an interrogation. How do you avoid this? Remember to reflect students' answers to open-ended questions. It both allows them to go deeper and also helps you avoid sounding like the School Resource Officer.

Student: "I need to get a B in Chemistry." *Change Talk*

Counselor: "What would you say is the biggest reason you need to get a B?" *Open-Ended Question*

Student: "All my friends are getting A's in the class. I have to at least make a B." *Change Talk*

Counselor: "You don't want to be embarrassed by getting less than a B." *Complex Reflection of Emotion*

Student: "Ya. I hate feeling embarrassed." *Change Talk*

You'll use both reflections and questions to encourage more Change Talk. The bottom line is that you want to be intrigued by Change Talk. When you hear it, you want to pounce on it. Use reflections and questions to help students consider what change would look like from every angle. The more they talk about change, the more likely they will make a lasting behavioral change.

Minimize or Ignore Sustain Talk

Our students, like all of us, are complicated beings. They're not going to spend an entire conversation only talking about reasons to change. Heck, they may not even spend one sentence only talking about change. Change Talk and Sustain Talk are usually muddled together. Students will switch back and forth or will even use both in one sentence. As we've said before, people are *ambivalent* about most things.

How are we supposed to respond to Sustain Talk? Remember that we don't want students to talk about keeping the status quo. That being the case, when we hear Sustain Talk, we can either reflect it as weakly as possible or even ignore it.

> **Student:** "My parents want me to get my grades up."

> **Counselor:** "They're putting the pressure on." ***Simple Reflection***

> **Student:** "Oh ya! But I don't really care about my grades, at least not like they do." ***Sustain Talk***

> **Counselor:** "What do you care about?"

In this example, the counselor ignores the student's Sustain Talk ("I don't really care about my grades") and, instead, asks the student about what he/she values. In doing so, the counselor distracts the student from talking more about the status quo. At the same time, the counselor is digging for value statements that can be reflected.

Oftentimes, Change Talk and Sustain talk will come at you in the same sentence.

> **Student:** "I want to get my grades up, but I just don't have that much time to study." ***Change Talk and Sustain Talk***

In a scenario like this, counselors should either only reflect the Change Talk or reflect both but always end with the Change Talk (as that's what the student is likely to elaborate on).

> **Counselor:** "It's important to you to get your grades up." ***Complex Reflection of Value***

> *or*

"You don't have a ton of time to study, and it's important to you to get your grades up." *Complex Reflection of Value*

Student: "Ya, I need to get at least a 3.0 so I get a discount on car insurance." *Change Talk*

Note that, when the counselor reflects both parts of the student's statement, he/she uses *and* instead of *but*. This is quite intentional. In MI, ambivalence is expected. That being the case, we acknowledge that two things can be true at once. In this case, the student both wants to get his/her grades up *and* doesn't think he/she has much time to study. Consider what would happen if the counselor used *but* like the student did.

Counselor: "You don't have a ton of time to study, but it's important to you to get your grades up."

Student: "Exactly. That's why I can't get my grades up even though I want to."

When we use *but*, we are encouraging students to see the world in impassable dichotomies. This student doesn't see a way out of these competing scenarios. The most likely outcome, then, is that the student will reluctantly stick with the status quo. However, when the counselor acknowledges that two seemingly opposing things can be true at the same time, he/she encourages more conversation that will likely lead to Change Talk and, eventually, behavior change.

The Spectrum of Change

Change usually doesn't happen as a result of one session (or any one thing, for that matter). Change is a journey, and it's a long road from the status quo to true behavior change. That being the case, we can't count unfettered change as the marker of success, at least in the short term. If we have a successful MI-driven session with an 11th-grader who wants to stop smoking weed, we can't expect that he/she will be clean the next time we meet with him/her. Change is a process, and any move toward positive change is a WIN.

It's helpful to think of change as a spectrum (see below). When students enter your office, they may be firmly entrenched in the status quo (1), or they may have taken a few small steps toward change (3). Your goal is not necessarily to catapult them to permanent change (10) in the span of a session or two. What we can do in a session or two is help compel them further down the spectrum, even if it's a small step. In other words, if the student who smokes weed every day before school skips smoking a day or two a month (a.k.a., moving from a 1 to a 2), good things are happening. We can celebrate that!

The Spectrum of Change

Status Quo   Some Change   Permanent Change

1   2   3   4   5   6   7   8   9   10

At the same time, don't be discouraged by Sustain Talk or actions that seem to be pointing students in the wrong direction. Because ambivalence is such a common human experience, it's perfectly normal for students to move up and down the spectrum. We can't get too up or too down, as our success does not depend on the ultimate outcome. Our job is to reflect what students want for themselves and set the stage as best we can for positive change.

Embracing the idea of change as a spectrum means we can have very short interactions with students that, if grounded in good MI practice, can have a meaningful impact. Having a 2-minute conversation in the hallway that includes a statement or two of Change Talk from the student could move him/her from a 2.5 to a 2.7. Success! This means we don't need 15 minutes with students in our offices to have an effect. We can be walking sources of change all day.

Counselor: "Hey Stacy!"

Student: "Hey Mrs. Williams!"

Counselor: "I remember your telling me that you wanted to get your math grade up. How's it going?"

Student: "Pretty well so far. I actually did my homework last night." ***Change Talk***

Counselor: "That's great! The last time we talked, you said you wanted to get your grade up because you wanted to make your parents happy. What do they think so far?"

Student: "My mom was so happy when she saw me working at the kitchen table last night. It made me want to keep trying." ***Change Talk***

Counselor: "Sounds like you love your mom a lot. So much you'll even do math to make her happy!" ***Complex Reflection of Emotion***

Student: "Exactly!"

Counselor: "Well, drop by my office sometime and let me know how it's going. See you later!"

Goal for the Week

Be *intrigued* by Change Talk. Train yourself to listen for it and jump all over it when you hear it. As you reflect Change Talk and ask for more of it, notice how much more students are thinking about and discussing change than they would have otherwise. You will be watching change happen before your eyes!

CHAPTER 5:

Fun with Change Talk!

As school counselors, what we care about more than anything is the well-being of our students. It's why we do what we do. We want them to have the best lives they possibly can, and that means making positive changes in their lives. The beautiful thing about MI is that it gives us the tools to help students make these changes happen!

There are 2 ways to know whether students are moving toward positive change: 1) whether they are using more and more Change Talk, and 2) whether they are using less and less Sustain Talk (Baer et al., 2008; Barnett et al., 2014; Gaume, Gmel, & Daeppen, 2008; Apodaca et al., 2014). In Chapter 4, we discussed the importance of using reflections and open-ended questions to encourage students to use more Change Talk. Those will be the most common ways you evoke Change Talk from your students, but they aren't the only ways. This chapter is full of activities you can use with students to increase Change Talk and help them think through what making a big life change would look like.

Five Questions to Grow Change Talk

One of the simplest ways to encourage students to discuss change is to have a few questions in your back pocket that you can use whenever they seem appropriate for the conversation. Below are 5 questions that naturally elicit Change Talk (Miller & Rollnick, 2013).

1. Why would you want to make this change?

2. How might you go about it in order to succeed?

3. What are the 3 best reasons for you to make this change?

4. How important is it for you to make this change and why?

5. What do you think you'll do?

You can use one of the questions when it fits nicely with a conversation you're already having, or you can ask students if they'd be interested in exploring change more by answering all 5 questions during a session. The beauty of using these questions is that you're more or less guaranteed to get Change Talk in the answers. You can then do what you know how to do - reflect the Change Talk and/or ask for more of it.

Change Rulers

Using Change Rulers (also called scaling questions) is a common MI technique, and for good reason - it works! The theory behind the use of Change Rulers is the idea that, to make a positive change, people have to believe that it is both *important* and that they are *able* to do it.

When using the Change Rulers, we're asking students how important the change is to them and how able they feel to make the change. We do this by using scaling questions in a particular way that evokes Change Talk.

> **Student:** "I want to do better in Mrs. Williams' class.
>
> **Counselor:** "You want to get a better grade in English. May I ask you something about that?" ***Simple Reflection and Asking Permission***
>
> **Student:** "Sure."
>
> **Counselor:** "On a scale of 1 to 10 with 1 being not important at all and 10 being the most important thing in the world to you, how important is it to get your grade up?" ***Change Ruler of Importance***
>
> **Student:** "Hmm...I'd say about a 6."
>
> **Counselor:** "Ok, so you're kind of in the middle. What makes you a 6 and not a 4?" ***Simple Reflection and Evoking Change Talk***
>
> **Student:** "I'm not a 4 because I want to be eligible to play on the basketball team." ***Change Talk***

Notice that the way the counselor encourages the student to use Change Talk is to ask why the student isn't a lower number on the ruler. It doesn't actually matter what number the student says they are. The key is to ask them why they're at that number and not a lower number. They can't help but give you reasons for change. Continuing the previous example...

Counselor: "Playing on the basketball team is a goal of yours." *Complex Reflection of Goal*

Student: "Ya, it's my favorite sport. I have to be passing English to be eligible to play." *Change Talk*

Counselor: "May I ask you another question about getting a better grade?" *Asking Permission*

Student: "Sure."

Counselor: "On a scale of 1 to 10, how confident do you feel in your ability to get a better grade in Mrs. Williams' class, with 1 being no confidence at all and 10 being complete certainty?" *Change Ruler of Ability*

Student: "About a 7."

Counselor: "Ok. And why are you a 7 and not a 5?"

Student: "I can pass the class. I just need to do my homework all the time." *Change Talk*

> **Counselor:** "You *know* you can pass. You just need to do your homework." ***Simple Reflection of Change Talk***

> **Student:** "Ya. If I have to do my homework to be eligible, I'll do it." ***Change Talk***

Querying Extremes

Querying extremes is a fancy way of saying counselors can ask students what would happen if they did/did not make the change they're considering. This is a way of letting students consider the effects of making or not making the change. Querying Extremes is especially useful with adolescents because they are not used to thinking far into the future. By asking these questions, counselors are likely asking students to consider things they haven't thought about yet. Here are some good Querying Extremes questions:

1. What would your life look like if you made/did not make this change?

2. What would you look forward to the most/least in the future if you did/did not make this change?

3. How would you like things to turn out for you in 5 years or so?

Some students will try to give you the "right" answer when you ask these types of questions. They will answer with what they expect an adult would say or what they think you want to hear. For example, when you're talking with students struggling with substance use, they might say, "If I don't change, my life will be really bad. That's why I'm going to 'Just Say No' next time!" The fact that you're talking with these students means they are ambivalent about change. If their answers don't sound that way, you can simply ask them if they're trying to give the "right" answer or if it's what they really believe. Most teens will bring the wall down once it's pointed out.

Another thing to think about when using these types of questions is the age of students with whom you're working. If you're talking with 4th graders, it may be difficult for them to think about what making/not making a change will be like in 5 years. For them, you could ask something like: *How would you like things to turn out for you by the end of the year?* Another consideration is whether you want to ask the question in the positive form (i.e., what it would be like to make the change), the negative form (i.e., what it would be like to not make the change), or both. In general, I like to stick with the positive form unless the student is far from change and is using a lot of Sustain Talk.

> **Counselor:** "You've mentioned that you want to fight less with your stepfather. May I ask you more about that?" ***Asking Permission***

> **Student:** "I guess."

> **Counselor:** "If you actually made that change, what would you be looking forward to most in the future as a result?" ***Querying Extreme***

Student: "I'm just tired of arguing every night. I want to be able to come home and relax and not have to worry about fighting." ***Change Talk***

Counselor: "It'd be such a relief to not have to be ready for an argument all the time." ***Complex Reflection of Emotion***

Two Roads

Two Roads is a visual aid counselors can use with students to help them think deeply about what lasting change would be like. In the process, students provide a ton of Change Talk. Here are the steps to the Two Roads activity:

1. Ask students for permission to do the activity.

2. On a piece of paper or a whiteboard, draw one road at the bottom of the page that diverges into two roads leading in different directions. Explain that one road represents making the change while the other represents not making the change.

3. Ask students to name the two roads. They can be as creative as they choose to be. Have students write the names next to the roads.

4. Ask students to mark where they are currently. They'll likely place themselves somewhere behind the fork in the road. Ask them why they put themselves in

the spot they chose and not further back. They'll likely respond with Change Talk.

5. Ask them what it would be like to take each of the two roads. They'll give you more Change Talk.

6. Ask students how far in the future they think the fork in the road is.

7. Ask them where all this leaves them.

The Two Roads activity does two powerful things - it requires that students use a ton of Change Talk, and it helps them think through the situation they're in. A nice by-product is that it also gives you a ton of information about their mindset concerning the proposed change as well as life in general.

> **Counselor:** "You've talked about getting in trouble less in class, but it hasn't happened so far. Would it be ok if we did a little activity to help you get a good feel for where you are with this decision?" *Asking Permission*

> **Student:** "Ya, I'm game."

> **Counselor:** *[after drawing the two roads]* "Ok, these two roads represent either doing what it takes to get into less trouble in class or not. The first thing I'm wondering is what you'd call these two paths. What are some good names

that would represent changing or not changing?"

Student: "Hmm...I think the one that isn't getting in trouble less would be called *Grounded Forever*. The other one would be called *The Right Thing*." *[student writes name next to each path]*

Counselor: "Ok, so we've got *Grounded Forever* and *The Right Thing*. Where would you say you are on our map right now?" ***Simple Reflection***

Student: *[student puts an X right before the roads diverge]* "I'd say I'm right about here."

Counselor: "It looks like you're pretty close to the fork in the road." ***Simple Reflection***

Student: "Ya, I think I need to make a decision really soon. Otherwise, I'm just going to get grounded over and over." ***Change Talk***

Counselor: "It sounds like you really hate being grounded. What would it be like to go down *The Right Thing* path?" ***Complex Reflection of Emotion***

Student: "I think the first thing I'd do is ask my teachers to move me away from my friends so I won't talk to them all the time. I would also have to remind myself to not talk to the new people around me. And I'd also start doing more of my

work in class instead of doing other stuff."
Change Talk

Counselor: "So, if you chose to go down this road, you'd be asking teachers to move you, you'd talk less to the new people around you, and you'd do more work in class. Let's think about this other road. What would happen if you went down *Grounded Forever?*" ***Simple Reflection***

Student: "Well, it would suck! I'd be sitting in my room every weekend, and I wouldn't get to hang out with anyone or play any video games. If I went further down that road, I'd probably not get to watch TV either. Eventually, my parents would probably just make me live out in the backyard!" ***Change Talk***

Counselor: "That sounds pretty terrible!" ***Complex Reflection of Emotion***

Student: "Ya! I don't want to be a weirdo who never gets to do anything or hang out with anyone." ***Change Talk***

Counselor: "You don't want to be bored and lonely." ***Complex Reflection of Emotion***

Student: "Heck no. That just can't happen."

Counselor: "So where does all this leave you?"

> **Student:** "I want to go down *The Right Thing* path! Well, I really don't because it's going to be hard. But it'll be worth it so that I'll have a life." ***Change Talk***

Talking Values

With the Talking Values activity, the goal is to help students identify their personal values and then consider whether their actions align with those values. Sadly, in most schools, it is very uncommon for students to have the opportunity to consider what their deeply-held beliefs are. It should be no surprise to us, then, that their lives don't reflect their values. This exercise helps students consider this for themselves and reflect on what making a change would look like.

To do this activity, you'll need some sort of list of values. This can be a simple list on paper or can be a deck of cards with various values written on them (values cards specific for teens can be found here: https://goo.gl/39pKeM). Either way, you'll want to make sure students know the definitions of the values, as these abstract concepts can be difficult to grasp for teens who rarely think about them. Here are the steps to this activity:

1. Ask students to look through the list of values and pick the 3 that matter most to them. Reiterate that you're asking about what they think, not what their family and friends think.

2. Ask students to put their top 3 values in order from most important to least important.

3. Ask students to talk about their current behaviors and how they relate to their top values.

4. It's important to normalize the fact that students' actions don't always reflect their values. That's true of us all. If you don't normalize this, students may get defensive.

5. Ask where this leaves students.

Here's an example from a conversation I had with a student earlier this year:

> **Counselor:** "Would it be alright with you if we do a little activity?" ***Asking Permission***

> **Student:** "Ya, sure."

> **Counselor:** "Ok, I want to think about what matters to you for a few minutes. I have this deck of cards with values on them. Would you be willing to look through them and pick out the 3 values that are most important to you?" ***Asking Permission***

> **Student:** "Ya, let's do it." *[student goes through deck and picks 3 cards]*

Counselor: "Alright, you picked loyalty, success, and family as your 3 top values." *Simple Reflection*

Student: "Ya, these are the 3 that stood out."

Counselor: "Ok, now let's put those 3 in order from most important to least important."

Student: "I think #1 would be success, #2 would be family, and #3 would be loyalty."

Counselor: "Success is what you value most, then family, and then loyalty. That's an important thing to know about yourself! If it's ok with you, I want to try and connect these things that are most important to you to what we were talking about the last time we met - that you're thinking about how much you've been smoking weed. Would that be ok?" *Simple Reflection and Asking Permission*

Student: "Ya, ok."

Counselor: "Great, thanks for being willing. Something you said last time just came to mind as we were talking about your values. You mentioned before that you're a little worried about how much you're using because it's been hurting your grades."

Student: "Ya, I remember that."

Counselor: "I'm wondering what you think about this situation where, on one hand, smoking may be hurting your grades, and, on the other hand, the most important value for you is success."

Student: "It's hard because I want to be successful, but I also like chillin' with my friends and smoking." *Change Talk and Sustain Talk*

Counselor: "You want to have fun with friends, and, at the same time, your ultimate value is success." *Complex Reflection of Value*

Student: "Ya, I have fun with my friends and all, but I eventually need to be successful so I can take care of my mom and maybe a wife and kids someday." *Change Talk*

Counselor: "You love your family and your future family a lot and want to take care of them. Like you said, family is your #2 value." *Complex Reflection of Emotion*

Student: "Ya, exactly."

Counselor: "It's a tough situation because the things you value most and your actions aren't always lining up. That's a common thing in a lot of people's lives."

Student: "I think it's part of growing up. I need to figure out what matters most to me and actually do it." *Change Talk*

Counselor: "It sounds like you're really considering making some changes." *Simple Reflection*

Summarizing

Summarizing is actually an advanced version of reflective listening. After several minutes of conversation with students, counselors can take a minute to summarize what they've heard to make sure they're understanding students correctly. In the process, counselors should focus the content of their summary on the Change Talk students have shared.

Summaries are great for 2 very important reasons: 1) students really feel heard because counselors are showing they've been listening intently for a while, and 2) counselors can frame the conversation around the Change Talk students have provided.

Summaries aren't just for the end of sessions. In fact, it's a very good idea to summarize a number of times during a session. More showing of empathy and reflection of Change Talk can't be bad! Here's a summary that continues the conversation in the example from the Talking Values section.

Counselor: "Would it be alright with you if I summarized what we've said so far to make sure I've got it?" ***Asking Permission***

Student: "Sure."

Counselor: "Ok. The last time we talked, you said a few things about maybe smoking less because you thought it might be hurting your grades. Today, we found out that what you value most is success, family, and loyalty. You mentioned that it's hard to stop smoking because it's a fun thing to do with your friends, and you're starting to realize that you need to make a change because it's more important to you to be successful and take care of your family. Do I have that about right?" ***Summary***

Here are a couple of things to take note of in this example: First, it's generally a good idea to ask for permission before you use a Summary. It will feel weird in the midst of the conversation otherwise, and, in asking for permission, you're validating students' autonomy. Second, notice how the counselor spends most of the summary on Change Talk. Also, he/she ends with Change Talk. In doing so, the counselor has framed the conversation such that it is firmly pointing in the direction of change. As the conversation continues, the student is likely going to continue talking about change. Finally, always end summaries by asking students if what you've said is accurate. Doing so helps avoid misunderstanding and, more importantly, reinforces their autonomy.

What to Think about Change Talk

When you start using the above techniques, it's tempting to get too excited about the Change Talk you hear. When Change Talk starts flowing, it's easy for us counselors to get too excited. You can't blame us - we want what's best for students, and when they start talking about positive change, we get pumped! Remember ambivalence, though. Just because students are using Change Talk doesn't mean they're ready to change their behavior. Moving from a 2 to a 4 on the Spectrum of Change isn't the same thing as moving to a 10.

Think about it this way: if a student you've worked with for years who has been failing classes for as long as you can remember says, "I want to make better grades", you may feel like the heavens have opened and angels are singing. Calm down. Just reflect the Change Talk and use the above skills to ask for more. Don't overplay your hand. If you jump up and down and start howling like your team won the Super Bowl, the student is likely to back off his/her statement. Whatever you do, *do not* start making plans about how the student will get his/her grades up. If you jump to planning too quickly, students will start using Sustain Talk or, worse, will start acting like they're going to change when they're not (we'll get to how to know when it's time to help students plan for change in Chapter 7).

On the other hand, what do you do if students start using Change Talk, but you don't believe them? For example, what do you do if the same student says he/she is going to make all A's next semester? Just go with it. Keep evoking more

Change Talk. The student will like that you're going there with him/her and not saying he/she can't do it.

> **Student:** "I've decided I'm going to make all A's next semester."

> **Counselor:** "You want to make all A's. Wow, that would be a huge change! What's appealing to you about making all A's?" ***Simple Reflection and Open-Ended Question***

The bottom line is, if in doubt, pursue more Change Talk. The more students talk about change, the more likely they are to make the change.

Goal for the Week

Try 2 of the activities from this chapter. Be nice to yourself by trying them out on students with whom you already have a good relationship. You can even tell them you're trying out a new activity and want their thoughts on it. If you don't already know of something they're thinking about changing, you can simply ask them. All of us want to make positive changes in our lives, and we're usually actively considering at least one change all the time.

CHAPTER 6:

Responding to Sustain Talk

In the previous chapter, we considered how to draw more Change Talk out of students and, in doing so, increase the likelihood they will make positive changes. As we mentioned previously, though, limiting Sustain Talk is just as important as increasing Change Talk (Baer et al., 2008; Apodaca et al., 2014). In fact, when it comes to adolescents, research seems to suggest that restraining Sustain Talk is even *more* important than increasing Change Talk (Baer et al., 2008). That being the case, we had better know how to effectively respond to Sustain Talk.

In Chapter 4, we learned that 2 ways of *shrinking* Sustain Talk are to ignore it or to reflect it as simply as possible. These will be your most-used weapons in the battle against the status quo. The goal is essentially to turn Sustain Talk into a dead end while growing Change Talk into a vast adventure.

> **Student:** "I hate Mrs. Jenkins' class, but I know I have to pass English to graduate."

> **Counselor:** "You know you need to pass English to get to your goal." ***Complex Reflection of Goal and Ignoring Sustain Talk***

> *or*

Counselor: "You don't like English class. What really matters to you, though, is graduating and all the possibilities that come with it." *Complex Reflection of Goal and Minimizing Sustain Talk*

In the above examples, the counselor either ignored the Sustain Talk entirely or reflected it as dully as possible while inviting the student to talk more about change (i.e., doing better in Mrs. Jenkins' class). Though these are the most common techniques to shrink Sustain Talk, there are others. In this chapter, we will look at a number of techniques that will help you limit Sustain Talk.

Double-Sided Reflection

A **Double-Sided Reflection** is a particular type of reflection in which counselors intentionally point out contradictions in students' thinking and ask them to explain. It's no surprise that students' actions and beliefs regularly contradict. Ambivalence is a normal part of life for us all. When we're trying to help students achieve positive change, though, a Double-Sided Reflection can help students address contradictions that may be holding them back.

A Double-Sided Reflection will typically take the form of "_____, yet _____". Here's an example from a conversation I had with a student a few weeks ago:

Student: "I decided last week that I don't want drama with that girl anymore."

Counselor: "You're sick of the drama." ***Complex Reflection of Emotion***

Student: "Ya. She's just isn't worth it."

Counselor: "How's it going so far?" ***Open-Ended Question***

Student: "It's been good. Today I went up to her and told her she's not worth all the drama she causes. She got all pissed and started yelling, so I told her how stupid she is."

Counselor: "Ok, help me out here. I'm a little confused by something you said. Today, you went up to her and told her she's not worth the effort, yet last week you decided you didn't want drama with her anymore. I'm a little confused by how those two things go together." ***Double-Sided Reflection***

The counselor points out the inconsistency in the student's plan and her actions. It's *vital* in a scenario like this that the counselor doesn't demean the student. For example, the counselor shouldn't say something like this:

Counselor: "*What?!* You decided you didn't want drama with the girl, but then you walked right up to her and started a fight. Why'd you do that?"

Although the counselor is pointing out the contradiction, he/she is doing it in a way that feels belittling to the student. In my experience, the best way to ensure you don't sound demeaning is to **Play Dumb**. As a counselor, you may have experienced a scenario in which a student finds himself/herself a thousand times over. You likely know exactly why a student isn't living up to what he/she decided. The best course of action, however, is usually to pretend you don't. There are a couple of reasons for this: 1) You may *not* know the actual reason for the contradiction. All students are different, and situations they experience are different. 2) The point is not that you understand what's going on. The important thing is that the student does. By playing dumb, you're letting the student process the situation. Going back to the previous example...

> **Counselor:** "Ok, help me out here. I'm a little confused by something you said. Today, you went up to her and told her she's not worth the effort, yet last week you decided you didn't want drama with her anymore. I'm a little confused by how those two things go together." ***Double-Sided Reflection***

> **Student:** "Well...I don't know. She just pisses me off!"

> **Counselor:** "Which is why you decided she's not worth it."

Student: "Exactly. Ugh. I just need to move on and find other people to be around." ***Change Talk***

In this example, the counselor reminds the student of the reason she wanted to make the change, and student responds by giving more Change Talk. The end result of the Double-Sided Reflection, then, is more Change Talk and less Sustain Talk.

Querying Extremes

In the last chapter, we talked about how Querying Extremes can be used to GROW Change Talk. This technique can also be used to *shrink* Sustain Talk. Here is an example:

Student: "My parents want me to get my grades up, but I just don't see the point." ***Sustain Talk***

Counselor: "What would your life look like in a year or two if you didn't change anything and kept going in the same direction?" ***Querying Extreme***

Student: "I don't know. I'm passing about half my classes right now, so I'd probably have to stay in high school an extra year. I'd be ok with that except that my friends will all be graduated." ***Change Talk***

> **Counselor:** "It would be lonely to still be here when your friends are graduated and gone."
> ***Complex Reflection of Emotion***

Using the Querying Extreme technique led the student to stop using Sustain Talk and actually use Change Talk.

Ask Why Someone Is Concerned

Oftentimes, we school counselors are talking about issues with students because other adults (parents, teachers, administrators, etc.) have brought them to our attention. From an MI perspective, this is definitely not ideal, as it is an affront to students' autonomy. However, it's also unavoidable. It can be awkward to call students into our offices and say something like, "____ told me you've been _____", as we are put in the position of cajoling for change, something that is diametrically opposed to MI practice. In my work with students, what I've found to be helpful is to 1) give away power (see Chapter 3), and 2) ask why someone is concerned.

> **Counselor:** "Thanks for coming down. I had someone bring up an issue to me that I want to ask you about. It might be a little awkward. Sorry about that. A staff member mentioned that he/she was concerned because you've been showing up to class under the influence of something."

> **Student:** "Who was it?"

Counselor: "Well, I can't share that information. You're not in trouble, though. Counselors don't do discipline. I'm asking because I care about you and how you're doing. You don't have to tell me anything if you don't want to. I'm just here to help you if you want it." ***Giving Away Power***

Student: "Nah, I don't think it's an issue. I use a little but not that much. I'm not worried about it." ***Sustain Talk***

Counselor: "You don't think it's an issue. It's your life and you can do whatever you want. May I ask you a question that came to my mind?" ***Giving Away Power and Asking Permission***

Student: "I guess."

Counselor: "I'm just wondering, if it's not a problem for you, how do you think someone noticed you were high? And were worried enough to tell me?" ***Asking Why Someone Is Concerned***

Student: "I don't know. Maybe I get a little carried away sometimes. I've used at lunch a time or two. I should probably stop doing that." ***Change Talk***

> **Counselor:** "Using at lunch could end up getting you in trouble, and you don't want that." ***Complex Reflection of Goal***

By taking the focus off the interaction between the counselor and the student and onto the event that raised concern, this technique usually opens the door to a decent conversation and even some Change Talk. In my experience, these kinds of conversations are some of the most awkward, but, if handled well, have led to some of my best working relationships with students.

Ask What Students Know

In the Bonus Material 1 section, we talked about how school systems have a generally unhelpful habit of using The Righting Reflex. Teachers, Administrators, and Counselors have a habit of lecturing students about how dangerous their actions are, how bad certain substances are, how much trouble cheating will get them into, etc. Unfortunately, this strategy almost never works because people listen to themselves, not other people. This technique takes advantage of that near-universal truth by having students explain what they know about the topic at hand. Here's a conversation I had with a student earlier this year:

> **Student:** "My mom is so annoying!"

> **Counselor:** "Something is frustrating you with your mom. What's going on?" ***Complex Reflection of Emotion***

Student: "She found out from one of my friends' moms that we've been smoking after school, and she freaked out like a crazy person."

Counselor: "She's really concerned, and it sounds like you're not." *Simple Reflection*

Student: "No, I'm not. She acts like we're meth addicts or something. We're just smoking a little." *Sustain Talk*

Counselor: "You don't think weed really affects you that much." *Simple Reflection*

Student: "No."

Counselor: "What do you know about how smoking affects people your age?" *Asking What Student Knows*

Student: "I guess I don't know that much. I mean I know it's not good for me. I just don't think it's that big a deal." *Change Talk and Sustain Talk*

Counselor: "You know it's not good for you." *Simple Reflection*

Student: "Well, I remember in health class the teacher saying something about it being bad for your brain when you're growing." *Change Talk*

Counselor: "It does something bad to your brain. What else do you know?" ***Asking What Student Knows***

Student: "I've heard it's bad for your lungs like smoking cigarettes is." ***Change Talk***

Counselor: "So it's probably bad for your brain in some way and also hurts your lungs. Have you ever seen bad things happen to people you know who smoke?" ***Asking What Student Knows***

Student: "I know this one guy. He smokes way more than I do. But he's pretty dumb. Seems like he's dumber than he was in middle school. I don't know - maybe that's because he smokes so much. I know I don't want to smoke as much as he does." ***Change Talk***

By asking students what they already know instead of hammering them with well-meaning lectures and guilt, we give them the chance to process the situation for themselves. When we ask them what they know, they're bringing into conscious thought what they passively know but do not actively consider.

Reflect What Isn't Said

When students are using a lot of Sustain Talk, they're being largely resistant to change. Though they may give off the opposite impression, most students are more ready to take steps in the right direction than they seem to be. One way to limit Sustain Talk and encourage Change Talk is to reflect what they're *not* saying.

Student: "My teacher sent me down because I don't do enough work in class."

Counselor: "Your teacher's concerned about how you're doing in her class." *Simple Reflection*

Student: "Ya."

Counselor: "How do you think it's going in her class?" *Open-Ended Question*

Student: "Fine." *Sustain Talk*

Counselor: "Even though your teacher is worried about you, you think everything's fine." *Simple Reflection*

Student: "Yep." *Sustain Talk*

Counselor: "You're not saying much. It seems like you don't really want to talk with me." *Reflecting What Isn't Said*

Student: "No, no. It's not that. I was just surprised she sent me down like that."

Counselor: "You were thrown off because she sent you down out of nowhere." ***Complex Reflection of Emotion***

Student: "Ya. I don't know why she had to do it like that. I don't really like how I'm doing in the class, but she could have brought it up a different way." ***Change Talk***

In this scenario, the student initially gives the impression that he is fine with his grade in the class and doesn't want to talk. In reality, though, he is just disoriented that his teacher sent him to the counselor out of the blue. By reflecting what the student hasn't said, the counselor is able to show empathy and also elicit Change Talk.

Sometimes, students know why they're in your office, but they avoid the topic. In this situation, it's usually helpful to point out the elephant in the room. Consider the below example in which a teacher has sent the student to the counseling office because she started yelling at another student in class. The teacher emailed the counselor beforehand to let him/her know the student was coming and why.

Counselor: "Hey, thanks for coming down. What's going on? How are you doing?" ***Open-Ended Question***

Student: "I'm good. I'm ready for the 3-day weekend coming up."

Counselor: "You're ready to have some extra time to relax." *Simple Reflection*

Student: "Ya, and I want to hang out with some friends. We'll probably go to the mall. Maybe a movie. What are you doing for the long weekend?"

Counselor: "I think I'll probably do some extra relaxing, too."

Student: "Cool. Hey, can we look at my schedule for next semester?"

Counselor: "Ya, we can do that in a few minutes. I'm noticing, though, that you haven't brought up why Mrs. Sanchez sent you to see me." *Reflecting What Isn't Said*

Student: "Ya, well I don't really want to talk about it. She was just upset because I told a girl what I thought about her."

Counselor: "The way you said something to another student made her nervous. Must have made a bit of a scene." *Simple Reflection*

Student: "Well I was pretty pissed. That girl drives me crazy on purpose!"

Counselor: "You were so mad you couldn't take it anymore." *Complex Reflection of Emotion*

Student: "Ya! Well that's what it felt like. But I probably could have waited until after class." ***Sustain Talk and Change Talk***

Counselor: "Even though you were furious, you probably could have waited to bring it up until later." ***Complex Reflection of Emotion***

Student: "Ya, probably. I probably would have been less pissed, too." ***Change Talk***

In this situation, the student isn't using Sustain Talk per se, but avoiding the topic has the same effect. By pointing out what the student isn't saying, the counselor gets the ball rolling toward Change Talk.

Shoot the Moon

Disclaimer: This technique is risky. Use with caution.

Shooting the Moon is a technique in which counselors over- or under-state what students are saying in order to point out its absurdity and evoke more realistic ideas. This can be a tricky strategy. I'd recommend only using it with students with whom you already have a strong relationship until you get the hang of it.

Student: "My parents are driving me crazy about grades. It's all they care about."

Counselor: "They're really frustrating you." ***Complex Reflection of Emotion***

Student: "Ya. It's ridiculous. I don't even care about my grades." *Sustain Talk*

Counselor: "You don't care about your grades at all." *Shooting the Moon*

Student: "Nope." *Sustain Talk*

Counselor: "You're ready to drop out, get a job in fast food, and live on minimum wage." *[counselor smiling]* *Shooting the Moon*

Student: "Well, maybe not that. I want to graduate. I even want decent grades. I just don't care as much as my parents." *Change Talk*

The nice thing about Shooting the Moon is that it can keep students from totally blocking Change Talk by using overblown Sustain Talk. With the right student, it's very useful because it cuts through the hyperbolic Sustain Talk so the conversation can move in a useful direction.

Shooting the Moon is risky for a couple of reasons. The first is that it generally requires sarcasm. Sarcasm isn't bad in and of itself, but it's usually off-putting to students if they misunderstand it. If you don't think the student you're working with will take your statements in jest, don't use them. Sarcasm is also hard to use with younger adolescents. It takes a decent grasp on abstract thought to correctly decode sarcasm.

The second danger with Shooting the Moon is that, occasionally, students will agree with your extreme statements. Going back to the previous example...

> **Counselor:** "You're ready to drop out, get a job in fast food, and live on minimum wage." *[counselor smiling]* **Shooting the Moon**

> **Student:** "Yep. I don't even care anymore."

Where can the counselor go from here? I like this technique and use it regularly. In my experience, it's rare that a student flatly agrees with my Shoot-the-Moon statements. When they do, what I typically do is acknowledge their autonomy.

> **Counselor:** "It's totally up to you. Your life doesn't belong to your parents. In the end, it's your life and you get to choose what to do with it. May I ask you something about that?" **Asking Permission**

> **Student:** "Ya, I guess."

> **Counselor:** "What do you want for your future - apart from your parents and teachers and anybody else?"

> **Student:** "I don't know yet. I'm thinking about going into healthcare. My parents don't understand that I don't need to go to a great university right away. I'm ok with going to community college at first."

> **Counselor:** "You're frustrated that they wouldn't listen to what you want." ***Complex Reflection of Emotion***

> **Student:** "Exactly!"

In a situation like this, students aren't usually frustrated at the counselor. If you can help them identify what they're upset about, you're likely to have a good conversation that isn't dominated by Sustain Talk.

Relationship Reluctance

When you're in situations where students are using a lot of Sustain Talk, it can feel like you're not connecting with them relationally. Students who are at 1 or 2 on the Spectrum of Change can come off as disliking you personally. This can be jarring to counselors, as we're accustomed to students liking us and enjoying the time they spend in our offices.

In my work with students, I've found that, when students give the impression they don't like me personally, the issue is really that they feel as though their autonomy is being threatened. Oftentimes, they were sent to my office against their will or their parents told them they had to make an appointment to talk with me. In scenarios like these, I focus on supporting students' autonomy until they feel comfortable enough to use the time the way they want to.

> **Student:** "I don't even know why I have to be here."

Counselor: "You *don't* have to be here. You can leave right now if you want. I'm here to help you if you want me to."

Student: "What can you do for me?"

Counselor: "Well, I don't know. It seems like Mrs. Mason thought I could help with something, but I'm here for you. I'm *your* counselor. What do you want to talk about?"

Student: "I didn't want to come down here at all."

Counselor: "You feel like you were forced to come here, and you don't want to be forced to do anything." ***Complex Reflection of Emotion***

Student: "Ya, I don't need people telling me what's good for me."

Counselor: "Well, I'm definitely not going to do that. I'm here to help with whatever *you* want help with."

Student: "I'm not worried about Mrs. Mason or her class. I don't have time for that."

Counselor: "Something else has been taking up your time." ***Simple Reflection***

Student: "Ya. I've been working a ton lately because my mom lost her job."

By respecting the student's autonomy, the counselor helps the student let go of his/her frustration about the situation and bring up what's really on his/her mind. If you'd like to see an example of a therapist deflecting a client's frustration with being required to meet with her, check out the particularly entertaining video at this link: https://goo.gl/1tt1cE

Every Little Bit Counts

As you're working with students who are not very motivated to change and are using a lot of Sustain Talk, remember the Spectrum of Change. Your goal is not to help them change their lives in a few minutes. They get to choose whether to change and when it happens. Sometimes, even with a world-class knowledge of all the techniques in the last few chapters, the best you can do is help move a student from a 2.0 to a 2.1. That's ok. In fact, that's success! Every little bit of change counts.

As school counselors, we rarely get to see the full extent of our work. We don't get to see that student with whom we worked for years finally 'get it' and excel in college. We don't get to see how working with a student on social skills in 6th grade helped him/her have a successful marriage 15 years later. The reality, though, is that every little bit of change matters. We are helping students plant seeds of positive change in their lives. Whether we get to see those seeds grow and flourish doesn't change the fact that we helped students plant them. What you do matters!

Goal for the Week

Try out 2 of these techniques this week. Challenge yourself by calling students down to your office who have been struggling in some area and will likely be resistant. This can be intimidating at first, but take courage! Learning these skills will lead to many lives changed in the future.

CHAPTER 7:

Commitment & Planning

You've shown students tons of empathy, built great working relationships, talked a lot about the change they're considering, and fought off the pesky Sustain Talk that occasionally returns. What's next? Some students (in my experience, the majority) will not need to make a plan with you - they'll simply change on their own. Other students will want your help creating a step-by-step change plan and executing that plan. In this chapter, we'll discuss how to know when students are ready to change and how to help them construct and follow a plan for long-term change.

Slow Down

Before we talk about how to test students' commitment to change and helping them make plans, I need to caution you to *not* move too quickly to this stage. Students are usually not ready to change as soon as you think they are. The reason? Ambivalence. Students will often sound like they're ready to charge out of your office and make sweeping life changes...but they're not.

You've probably already experienced this plenty of times. You have great conversations with students about getting their grades up, they seem really committed to it, and you feel great about yourself as a counselor...and then they come back two weeks later with worse grades than when they left.

How could this happen?!? Sometimes students felt the pressure to say what they think you want to hear, while others genuinely thought they'd change ...but don't. The bottom line is they weren't ready to change yet.

In both my own experience using MI and in training other counselors to use MI, the most common mistake is pushing students to change when they're not ready. It's a very subtle problem that happens before counselors even notice.

> **Counselor:** "What makes you want to find another group to sit with at lunch?"

> **Student:** "A lot of things. I need some new friends. I'm sick of getting in trouble with my old group, and there's so much drama." ***Change Talk***

> **Counselor:** "What are you going to do today to find another group?" ***Planning***

It's *so* easy to start the planning phase before students are actually ready. The student in this example will answer with action items; he/she isn't going to say, "I don't know if I'm ready yet." The counselor won't know the student wasn't fully committed until later when he/she finds out that the student didn't follow through with the plan. This kind of scenario replays itself zillions of times in counseling offices everywhere. It's a frustrating situation for all involved because the student usually feels embarrassed, the counselor feels as though he/she did something wrong, and an opportunity to pursue Change Talk was squandered. If this scenario happens a few times with the same student, he/she may pull away from the counselor relationally because he/she can't bear the negative feelings associated with letting the counselor down.

So what do we do to avoid situations like this? In two words, **slow down**. Talk is cheap. Just because students use a lot of Change Talk in a given session doesn't mean they're ready to actually change. Usually, it takes quite a bit of discussing the emotions, goals, and values associated with a change before students are really ready. Said another way, try to resist talking about *how* to change and keep pushing the conversation toward *why* to change. Here's how the previous example could have gone...

> **Counselor:** "What makes you want to find another group to sit with at lunch?"

> **Student:** "A lot of things. I need some new friends. I'm sick of getting in trouble with my old group, and there's so much drama." *Change Talk*

> **Counselor:** "All the drama is really weighing you down." *Complex Reflection of Emotion*

> **Student:** "Ya, the other day, we spent all of lunch arguing about who liked this one guy more than everybody else. It was stupid." *Change Talk*

Counselor: "That kind of stuff happens often, and it really annoys you." ***Complex Reflection of Emotion***

Student: "Ya. I just want to eat lunch and have fun." ***Change Talk***

In this example, instead of barreling ahead to planning, the counselor evokes more Change Talk. The more Change Talk the student uses, the more committed he/she becomes. And the more committed he/she is, the more likely real behavior change will happen, regardless of whether the counselor plans it with the student.

How Do We Know When Students Are Ready To Plan?

How can we know when students are really ready to plan for change? Are you ready for an annoying answer? We *can't*. All students are different, and they show their readiness to plan in different ways. The reality is that you probably won't know the exact moment when students are ready to start making behavior changes. Bummer.

Here is the *great* news, though: students don't need to plan with you to make changes. The vast majority of students will start making behavior changes without talking with you beforehand. Most students will talk with you about why they want to change (Change Talk) and will walk out of your office and start making changes on their own. This makes total sense because the power of MI comes from *within* students. When properly motivated, most students don't need help knowing how to change - they'll figure it out!

Consider the previous example. Most students don't need our help knowing how to make new friends. What they need help with is tapping into their internal motivation to do it.

This idea is a pretty radical shift in mindset for most counselors. We feel useful when we're helping students make concrete plans to do something, whether it's to make new friends, increase grades, improve their relationship with their parents, or apply to a particular university. The problem is that students can make plans all day long, but if they're not actually ready to make the change, they won't do it when the rubber meets the road. Counselors impact most students' lives far more when we help them consider *why* to make a change instead of *how*. It's a hard shift for many counselors because, frankly, it's hard to trust that students will follow through on change. We feel better about it if they have a practical, step-by-step plan for change. Unfortunately for us, plans don't come to life unless they're built on resolute motivation. I have found that, for many counselors, the hardest part about using MI is truly trusting that students will pursue change on their own once they've fully processed the ambivalence that has been holding them back.

In my experience using MI, about 90% of my students walk out of my office and make change happen on their own. Sometimes, we've met for 5 minutes, sometimes 4 or 5 sessions of 15 minutes each. I don't know when it happens, but, at some point, students make the decision that they're ready to change. Oftentimes, they'll visit me months later to tell me their grades are up, they're hanging out with new friends, they're using less substances, they got out of a bad relationship, etc. I didn't plan a thing with them. I simply helped them think about *why* to change.

Consider one of the first study ever done on MI (Miller, Sovereign, & Krege, 1988). Miller, one of the creators of MI, hypothesized that, if he used MI for 15 minutes with alcoholics, they'd be more likely to sign up for an in-patient treatment program. He was sad to find out that, in fact, there was no difference in how frequently people who received MI signed up for treatment. Miller was ready to give up on the idea of MI, thinking the techniques must not work as well as he thought. However, he contacted the clients who took part in the study a year later to check in with them and found that a significant number of people who received the initial MI session had quit cold turkey! They didn't sign up for the treatment program because they didn't think they needed it. They just walked out of Miller's office after 15 minutes of MI and, being fully motivated to quit, figured it out on their own. For those of you who have family members or friends who struggle with addiction, you know how amazing these results really are. People struggling with addiction are notoriously difficult to motivate to change and to help actually kick the habit. If 15 minutes of MI can help addicts quit on their own without a plan, surely we can trust that MI can help motivate many of our students to change of their own accord.

Testing the Water

For those students who want to make a plan with us, how do we know when they're ready to move from talking about change to actually making steps toward change? One thing we can do is to **Test the Water** with certain questions (Naar-

King & Suarez, 2011). To Test the Water, start by using a Summary to remind students what you've discussed thus far in your session(s). Then, use a **Test the Water Question** to see how ready students are to plan. Here are some Test the Water Questions I like to use:

1. Where does this leave you?

2. Where do you think you'll go from here?

3. What's the next step for you?

4. If you were going to take the next step toward [change], what would it look like?

Here is what a conversation using a Testing the Water question might sound like:

> **Counselor:** "Would it be ok if I summarized what we've said so far to make sure I have it right?"
>
> **Student:** "Ya, sure."
>
> **Counselor:** "Ok. For most of your time in middle school and high school, you had no idea what you wanted to do for a career. At some point, you just decided you weren't going to worry about it. Things changed recently, though, because you talked to your uncle about his career as an electrician, and a lot about what he

does sounds good to you. You like that he doesn't have to sit at a desk all day, that he gets to be a part of building things, and, most of all, you like that he makes good money. Since then, you've been thinking about what it would be like to be an electrician. Is that about right?" ***Summary***

Student: "Ya, that sounds about right. Oh, and I forgot to tell you that my uncle was at the house this weekend and told me that he got into the field by doing an internship." ***Change Talk***

Counselor: "Where does all of that leave you?" ***Testing the Water***

Student: "I think the next step for me is to talk to my uncle more and figure out how to do an internship." ***Change Talk***

This part of the process is called Testing the Water because we don't know for sure whether students are ready to start acting on their desire to change. As we've said, with most students, they sound ready to change before they actually are. They'll use a lot of Change Talk before they're ready to actually act on their desire. That being the case, don't be discouraged if they aren't ready to act quite yet. You'll know they're not ready if you hear Sustain Talk when you Test the Water. Here's what that might sound like in the previous example:

Student: "Ya, that sounds about right. Oh, and I forgot to tell you that my uncle was at the house this weekend and told me that he got into the field by doing an internship." *Change Talk*

Counselor: "Where does all of that leave you?" *Testing the Water*

Student: "I don't know. An internship sounds ok, but I'm just still not sure being an electrician is for me." *Sustain Talk*

If students aren't ready to act on their desire to change yet, that's ok! Just keep drawing Change Talk from them by using the skills in Chapter 5 until they are ready. In the previous example, the counselor could say something like...

Counselor: "You're not sold on being an electrician quite yet, and, at the same time, you're seeing the importance of having a plan for your future career." *Double-Sided Reflection*

Student: "Ya, I don't know if I want to be an electrician, but I want to have a plan for what to do when I graduate." *Change Talk*

One word of caution: *never* tell students they're ready to change. In an effort to encourage students, some counselors make the mistake of saying something like, "You're ready to bring your grades up. You can do this!" Don't say things like that. If you have to tell students they're ready, they're not ready.

Planning

When you're working with students who show they're ready to make a plan, resist the temptation to take control of the conversation (beware of the Righting Reflex). Instead, use the skills you've already learned (i.e., Simple Reflection, Open-Ended Questions, Complex Reflections, Asking Permission, etc.). Below are steps to making a plan using MI principles. *Disclaimer: There is no one way to make a plan. These are suggested steps. You can use any combination any number of times.*

Ask Permission - As with other aspects of MI, it's always important to ask for permission. This is especially true if students haven't brought up making a plan, and you're choosing to float the idea.

> **Counselor:** "What do you think about coming up with a plan to help you start making this change?" *Asking Permission*

> **Student:** "Ya, that sounds good."

Set a Change Goal - At this point, you've probably talked at length about the change students want to make. However, you've also talked about it in a lot of different ways - why it makes sense emotionally, why it aligns with students' goals/values, how it would look in everyday life, how confident they are, etc. That's why it's important for students to put their big-picture change goal into words before they begin planning how to tackle the challenge of changing.

> **Counselor:** "A plan sounds like it would be helpful to you." *Simple Reflection*

> **Student:** "Ya, it does."

> **Counselor:** "Ok, before we start making a plan, how would you put into words what your overall goal is?" *Open-Ended Question*

> **Student:** "Um...I would say my goal is to finish 7th grade with 2 A's." *Setting a Change Goal*

> **Counselor:** "It's important to you to finish the year with 2 A's." *Complex Reflection of Goal*

Pick Specific Steps - After setting the big-picture change goal, it's helpful to break it into manageable parts. This looks different depending on the student. Some like to make a list of all the steps leading toward the goal, whereas others only want to discuss the first step or two. As you'd expect, this is heavily affected by the student's age and maturity level. The bottom line is that this part of the process is unique to each student. Below are some things that have helped my students as they've created steps toward change:

Be Specific - Help students choose goals that are as specific as possible. For example, "getting my grades up" isn't specific enough because it's something students like to say to make adults happy, but it isn't quantifiable. If students really want to bring their grades up, you could recommend they choose a certain amount of increase after a certain amount of time. That way, it's easy to tell how students are doing on their path toward change.

> **Counselor:** "What do you think about picking a step or two that are specific enough that we can tell if you've completed them by next week?"

Choose Imminently Doable Steps - Make goals very doable, especially early in the process. When students feel very motivated (which they will because of all that great MI work you've done with them), they often pick unrealistic goals. This is a bad idea. Rome wasn't built in a day, and engrained behaviors usually aren't changed overnight. When students are beginning their trek toward lasting change, it's helpful to pick goals that will be easy for them to accomplish. That way, they're encouraged when they succeed and are excited to move on to the next step.

> **Counselor:** "Instead of trying to get all your grades up to A's by next week, what do you think about trying to turn in that one science assignment you're missing by next week?"

Discuss Roadblocks Beforehand - Some students are very excited about their first steps toward positive change...until they hit roadblocks. Adversity is quite the momentum killer *unless* students see it coming. Counselors can help students think through things that will make change difficult before they experience them in real life. One thing to note: talking about roadblocks is essentially Sustain Talk. That being the case, don't discuss them until you're sure students are deeply motivated to change, and finish the discussion with a heavy dose of Change Talk.

> **Counselor:** "You're ready to cut back on how much you smoke. What do you think will make that hard this week?"

Whiteboard Plans - I love using the whiteboard in my office. Because adolescents aren't very good at abstract thought, it's helpful for them to get their thoughts out of the brains and onto the board (if you don't have a whiteboard, markers and paper work just fine). This is especially true when they're creating change plans. You can have students make lists of reasons to change, write out their goals for the week, outline potential roadblocks, etc. Some students like to draw things out while others prefer to create bulleted lists. Whatever works for them is just fine. When they're done, I always have my students take a picture with their phones so they can look back on their plans during the week and we can reference it during our next session.

Role-Play - For many students, it is beneficial to role-play certain scenarios they'll face as they oppose the status quo. Sometimes, this can mean role-playing an actual conversation while at other times it can mean playing out an internal dialogue.

> **Counselor:** "It sounds like you're going to be faced with some scenarios this week when you're going to have to make different decisions.

What do you think about working through one of those times to help you get ready?"

Student: "Ya, that sounds fine."

Counselor: "Ok, you said your goal for this week is to cut back to playing video games for 1 hour a day. Would it be ok if we thought through what it will be like to shut off the Xbox after an hour?"

Student: "Ok, sure."

Share Plans with Someone - We school counselors are influential parts of students' lives, no doubt! However, our influence is minimal when compared to people who spend hours per day with a given student - parents, grandparents, best friends, etc. One thing that has been helpful for my students is to share their change plan with someone they trust to hold them accountable.

Counselor: "You're feeling really good about doing your Spanish homework every night. What do you think about telling someone about your goal? Someone who you trust to help you if you need it?"

Student: "Ya, I think that's a good idea."

Counselor: "You'd like to have some back-up." *Simple Reflection*

Student: "Ya, I think I will talk to my friend who's in the same class. Maybe we could even do our homework together."

Follow Up - It's generally a good idea to follow up with students in a relatively short amount of time, particularly when they're just venturing out on their journey toward lasting change. The timeframe is different based on the student and the goal, but I typically check back in a few days to a week. Sometimes I will propose the timing I think is best while, at others times, I will let students decide.

Counselor: "I'm excited to hear how it goes! When do you want me to check in with you to see what I can do to help?"

Celebrate Success and Bring Grace to Shortcoming - When we check in, it's important that we truly *celebrate* students' success. I typically exaggerate my celebrations to the point of making them wonder why I'm so happy. They pretend to think I'm crazy, but they actually love being bragged on!

Student: "Well, I didn't have any fights with my parents last week."

Counselor: "WOW!! That's amazing! You did it! You did exactly what you were hoping to do."

Student: "Ya, it was nice to not have to worry about it." ***Change Talk***

Counselor: "It was a relief to not have to fix issues after a fight." ***Complex Reflection of Emotion***

Student: "Ya, exactly."

Counselor: "Can I brag on you for a second?" ***Asking Permission***

Student: "Um...ok."

Counselor: "It's not easy to make a big change like that, especially when your parents are involved. I think it says a ton about you that you were able to accomplish your plan for last week."

When students aren't able to fulfill their plan, it's even more important that we invite them to offer themselves grace. Changing is hard business, and it's ok to stumble along the way.

Student: "I really thought I could not smoke for a week, but I ended up doing it. All my friends got together this weekend. All they were doing was smoking, so I did, too."

Counselor: "You're pretty disappointed that you didn't accomplish your goal." ***Complex Reflection of Emotion***

Student: "Ya. I just thought I would be able to do it."

Counselor: "Because it's important to you to smoke less."

Student: "Ya, I really want to quit. I need to be healthier." *Change Talk*

Counselor: "Would it be ok if I share a thought about all this?" *Asking Permission*

Student: "Sure."

Counselor: "Making a big, important change like this is hard. Really hard! There's *no shame* in slipping up along the way."

Return to Reasons for Change - When you're following up with students, regardless of whether they fulfill their short-term steps toward change, return to their reasons for change. In other words, keep drawing out emotions, goals, and values that motivate them to change. Remind them of reasons they've given in the past and delve into them more deeply. Ambivalence is always lurking. The power of MI is in helping students remind themselves why they want to change.

Plans are Overrated

It's ironic that this is one of the longer chapters in the book because planning is the *least* important aspect of MI. Most of the time, students will know what they need to do to change. When you help them realize what is motivating them to change, they'll do it on their own. They know what to do; they just need help motivating themselves to do it. This is true for most of us. We all know how to lose weight, eat healthier, work out more, read more books, spend more quality time with friends, (fill in new year's resolution here)...we just don't do it because we aren't sufficiently motivated. The same is true for most of our students. Raising grades, avoiding trouble, making healthy decisions, and so on isn't rocket science. It just takes a ton of motivation! All that is to say, don't focus on planning. The vast majority of students will be more well-served by considering reasons *why* they want to change than *how* they're going to do it.

Goal for the Week

Try using a Test the Water Question with a student with whom you've been working for a while. If they seem ready, start making some plans!

BONUS MATERIAL 3:

MI Cheat Sheet

MI = Empathy + Change Talk

EMPATHY

Simple Reflections

Reflect a few words or ideas shared by the student

Complex Reflections

Emotions – *"You're feeling..."*

Goals – *"A goal of yours is..."*

Values – *"It's important to you that..."*

Autonomy & Asking Permission

Give Away Power Phrases/Questions- *"It's totally up to you. It's your life..."*

Asking Permission: *"Would it be ok if I...?"*

CHANGE TALK

GROW Change Talk, *shrink* **Sustain Talk**

Be Intrigued by Change Talk: Reflect it, Ask questions about it

Ignore/Minimize Sustain Talk

Strategies to GROW Change Talk

5 Questions, Change Rulers, Querying Extremes, Two Roads, Talking Values, Summarizing

Strategies to *shrink* **Sustain Talk**

Double-Sided Reflection, Querying Extremes, Ask Why Someone Is Concerned, Ask What Students Know, Reflect What Isn't Said, Shoot the Moon

Test the Water & Planning

Testing the Water Questions - *"Where does this leave you?"*

Planning - Ask Permission, Set a Change Goal, Pick Specific Steps, Follow Up, Celebrate Success & Bring Grace to Shortcoming, Return to Reasons for Change

Conclusion:

You're Changing Lives!

Focus on the Why

There you have it! Seven chapters on how to do Motivational Interviewing. It's that easy! Actually, it's not at all. As you're stumbling around with new skills, getting headaches from trying to figure out what to say next, and waiting to see results, remember *why* you want to learn to use MI. In the same way that you help students focus on the why, do it yourself as well.

If you've gotten to the end of this book and are trying to learn these new skills, I have a pretty good idea why you're doing it: you care deeply about your students and want to help them. When learning MI gets difficult or you have a rough day at the office because you're dealing with pain in students' lives, remember why you do what you do. Help yourself tap into your own emotions, goals, and values.

Lives Changed

MI works. Used properly, it will help students change their lives. You won't always get to see how students' lives are changed, but sometimes you will...and it will be awesome! In reality, though, it isn't MI that changes lives. MI is a tool. When we see a great work of art, we don't celebrate the paint brush or the hammer and chisel - we honor the artist.

With MI, students are the artists accessing the beauty within themselves and molding their lives into the expression they want it to be. School counselors are their assistants, helping them throw open the doors to their hearts.

Thank you for what you do, school counselors. Thank you for caring for students' hearts. Thank you for helping them tap into their fullest potential. Thank you for caring about your craft enough to invest in your own skills. You're changing lives, and you're changing the world.

Next Steps

How Do I Get Really Good at MI?

This is going to seem mean... several research studies show that reading a book doesn't actually make people good at MI long-term (Miller & Mount, 2001; Miller, Yahne, Moyers, Martinez, & Pirritano, 2004; Hall, Staiger, Simpson, Best, & Lubman, 2016). It's just the first step. According to the creators, becoming an MI expert typically looks something like this:

1. Read a book about MI

2. Attend a 2-day beginner workshop/receive individual training

3. Attend a 2-day advanced workshop/receive individual training

4. Receive individual coaching from an MI trainer

The above studies show that reading a book and doing the beginning and advanced workshops or comparable trainings help people become proficient in MI for a while. Over time, though, their skills diminish. It isn't until people receive individual coaching that their skills persevere long-term. After I learned about MI and read Miller and Rollnick's book (2013), I spent my own money to travel to a place where 2-day workshops were offered. However, it wasn't until I received individual coaching that I felt truly proficient in MI.

I have since seen similar outcomes with folks I have trained/coached in MI.

If you're interested in taking further steps to become an MI expert and think I could help you and/or folks in your building or district with training or coaching, please contact me! My email address is MIforSchoolCounselors@gmail.com.

MI Research

There is a *ton* of research supporting the use of MI in about as many situations as you can imagine. Below is a handful of research articles providing evidence that MI is effective in areas most relevant to school counselors. This is a *tiny* percentage of all the studies supporting MI.

MI Works in Addiction Treatment

Smoking (Bolger et al., 2010; Harris et al., 2010)

Alcohol (Baer, Kivlahan, Blume, McKnight, & Marlett, 2001; Burke, Da Silva, Vaughan, & Knight, 2005; Scholl & Schmitt, 2009; Tevyaw et al., 2007)

Marijuana (Swan et al., 2008; Walker et al., 2006)

MI Works with Adolescents

Smoking (Peterson et al., 2009)

Marijuana (D'Amico, Miles, Stern, & Meredith, 2008)

Conduct problems (Greenwald, 2002)

Eating disorders (Gowers et al., 2007)

MI Works in Schools

Preventing secondary school dropout (Atkinson & Woods, 2003)

Reducing truancy (Enea & Dafinoiu, 2009)

Improving study habits and grade performance (Daugherty, 2009)

Classroom management (Reinke, Herman, & Sprick, 2001)

Handling disciplinary referrals (Kelly & Lapworth, 2006; LaBrie, Lamb, Pedersen, & Quinlan, 2006)

Increasing grades (Strait et al., 2012; Terry, Smith, Strait, & McQuillin, 2013; Terry, Strait, McQuillin, & Smith, 2014)

References

American School Counselor Association. (2011). Student-to-school-counselor ratio 2010-2011. Retrieved from https://www.schoolcounselor.org/asca/media/asca/home/Ratios10-11.pdf

American School Counselor Association. (2012). ASCA national model: A framework for school counseling programs (3rd ed.). Alexandria, VA: Author.

Armstrong, M. J., Mottershead, T. A., Ronksley, P. E., Sigal, R. J., Campbell, T. S., & Hemmelgarn, B. R. (2011). Motivational interviewing to improve weight loss in overweight and/or obese patients: A systematic review and meta-analysis of randomized controlled trials. Obesity Reviews, 12, 709–723. doi:10.1111/j.1467-789X.2011.00892.x

Apodaca, T. R., Borsari, B., Jackson, K. M., Magill, M., Longabaugh, R., Mastroleo, N. R., & Barnett, N. P. (2014). Sustain talk predicts poorer outcomes among mandated college student drinkers receiving a brief motivational intervention. Psychology Of Addictive Behaviors, 28(3), 631-638. doi:10.1037/a0037296

Atkinson, C., & Woods, K. (2003). Motivational interviewing strategies for disaffected secondary school students: A case example. Educational Psychology in Practice, 19(1), 49-64.

Baer, J. S., Beadnell, B., Garrett, S. B., Hartzler, B., Wells, E. A., & Peterson, P. L. (2008). Adolescent change language within a brief motivational intervention and substance use outcome. Psychology of Addictive Behaviors, 22, 570-575.

Baer, J. S., Kivlahan, D. R., Blume, A. W., McKnight, P., & Marlatt, G. A. (2001). Brief intervention for heavy-drinking college students: 4-year follow-up and natural history. American Journal of Public Health, 91(8), 1310-1316.

Bandura, A. (2002). Social cognitive theory of mass communication. In J. Bryant & M. B. Oliver (Eds.), Media effects: Advances in theory and research (pp. 94-124). New York, NY: Routledge.

Barnett, E., Moyers, T. B., Sussman, S., Smith, C., Rohrbach, L. A., Sun, P., & Spruijt-Metz, D. (2014). From counselor skill to decreased marijuana use: Does change talk matter? Journal of Substance Abuse Treatment, 46(4), 498-505. doi:10.1016/j.jsat.2013.11.004

Bolger, K., Carter, K., Curtin, L., Martz, D. M., Gagnon, S. G., & Michael, K. D. (2010). Motivational interviewing for smoking cessation among college students. Journal of College Student Psychotherapy, 24(2), 116-129.

Burke, P. J., Da Silva, J. D., Vaughan, B. L., & Knight, J. R. (2005). Training high school counselors on the use of motivational interviewing to screen for substance abuse. Substance Abuse, 26(3-4), 31-34.

Clark, C. (2011). Hurt 2.0: Inside the world of today's teenagers. Grand Rapids, MI: Baker.

Clark, M. D. (2014, March 23). As need for school counselors grow, numbers decrease. USA Today. Retrieved from http://www.usatoday.com/story/news/nation/2014/03/23/as-need-for-school-counselors-grows-numbers-decrease/6759591/

Connell, A. M., & Dishion, T. J. (2008). Reducing depression among at-risk early adolescents: Three-year effects of a family-centered intervention embedded within schools. Journal of Family Psychology, 22(4), 574-585.

D'Amico, E. J., Miles, J. N. V., Stern, S. A., & Meredith, L. S. (2008). Brief motivational interviewing for teens at risk of substance use consequences: A randomized pilot study in a primary care clinic. Journal of Substance Abuse Treatment, 35(1), 53–61. doi: 10.1016/j.jsat.2007.08.008

Daugherty, M. D. (2009). A randomized trial of motivational interviewing with college students for academic success. Doctoral dissertation, University of New Mexico, Albuquerque. Retrieved from http://libproxy.unm.edu/login?url=http://search.ebsc ohost.com/login.aspx?direct=true&db=psyh&AN=2009 -99060-447&login.asp&site=ehost- live&scope=site.

Elliott, R., Bohart, A.C., Watson, J.C., & Greenberg, L.S. (2011). Empathy. In J. Norcross (Ed.), Psychotherapy relationships that work (2nd ed.) (pp. 132-152). New York: Oxford University Press.

Enea, V., & Dafinoiu, I. (2009). Motivational/solution-focused intervention for reducing school truancy among adolescents. Journal of Cognitive and Behavioral Psychotherapies, 9(2), 185-198.

Feldstein Ewing, S. W., Filbey, F. M., Sabbineni, A., Chandler, L. D., & Hutchinson, K. E. (2011). How psychological alcohol interventions work: A preliminary look at what fMRI can tell us. Alcoholism: Clinical and Experimental Research, 35(4), 643-651.

Gaume, J., Gmel, G., & Daeppen, J. B. (2008). Brief alcohol interventions: Do counsellors' and patients' communication characteristics predict change? Alcohol and Alcoholism, 43(1), 62–69. http://doi.org/10.1093/alcalc/agm141

Gowers, S. G., Clark, A. W., Roberts, C., Griffiths, A., Edwards, V., Bryan, C., Smethurst, N., Byford, S., & Barrett, B. (2007). Clinical effectiveness of treatments for anorexia nervosa in adolescents: Randomised controlled study. British Journal of Psychiatry, 191, 427– 435.

Greenwald, R. (2002). Motivation-Adaptive Skills-Trauma Resolution (MASTR) therapy for adolescents with conduct problems: An open trial. Journal of Aggression, Maltreatment, & Trauma, 6(1), 237–261. doi:10.1300/J146v06n01

Hall, K., Staiger, P. K., Simpson, A., Best, D., & Lubman, D. I. (2016). After 30 years of dissemination, have we achieved sustained practice change in motivational interviewing? Addiction 111(7), 1144-1150 doi: 10.0000/add.13014

Harris, K. J., Catley, D., Good, G. E., Cronk, N. J., Harrar, S., & Williams, K. B. (2010). Motivational interviewing of smoking cessation in college students: A group randomized controlled trial. Preventive Medicine, 51(5), 387-393.

Herman, K. C., Reinke, W. M., Frey, A. J., & Shepard, S. A. (2014). Motivational interviewing in schools. New York, NY: Springer.

Horvath, A. O., & Symonds, B. D. (1991). Relation between working alliance and outcome in psychotherapy: A meta-analysis. Journal Of Counseling Psychology, 38(2), 139-149. doi: 10.1037/0022-0167.38.2.139

Kelly, A. B., & Lapworth, K. (2006). The HYP program: Targeted motivational interviewing for adolescent violations of school tobacco policy. Preventive Medicine, 43(6), 466-471.

LaBrie, J. W., Lamb, T. F., Pedersen, E. R., & Quinlan, T. (2006). A group motivational interviewing intervention reduces drinking and alcohol-related consequences in adjudicated college students. Journal of College Student Development, 47(3), 267-280.

Lambert, M. J., & Barley, D. E. (2001). Research summary on the therapeutic relationship and psychotherapy outcome. Psychotherapy: Theory, Research, Practice, Training, 38(4), 357-361. doi:10.1037/0033-3204.38.4.357

Mayo Clinic Staff. (2016). Cognitive behavioral therapy [Web page]. Retrieved from http://www.mayoclinic.org/tests-procedures/cognitive-behavioral-therapy/details/what-you-can- expect/rec-20188674

Miller, W. R., & Baca, L. M. (1983). Two-year follow-up of bibliotherapy and therapist-directed controlled drinking training for problem drinkers. Behavior Therapy, 14(3), 441-448.

Miller, W. R., Benefield, R. G., & Tonigan, J. S. (1993). Enhancing motivation for change in problem drinking: A controlled comparison of two therapist styles. Journal of Consulting and Clinical Psychology, 61(3), 455-461. doi:10.1037/0022-006X.61.3.455

Miller, W. R., & Mount, K. (2001). A small study of training in motivational interviewing: Does one workshop change clinician and client behavior? Behavioural and Cognitive Psychotherapy, 29, 457-471.

Miller, W. R., Sovereign, R. G., & Krege, B. (1988). Motivational interviewing with problem drinkers: II. The Drinker's Check-up as a preventive intervention. Behavioural Psychotherapy, 16, 251-268.

Miller, W. R., & Rollnick, S. (2013). Motivational interviewing: Helping people change (3rd ed.). New York, NY: Guilford.

Miller, W. R., Taylor, C. A., & West, J. C. (1980). Focused versus broad-spectrum behavior therapy for problem drinkers. Journal of Consulting and Clinical Psychology, 48(5), 590-601. doi:10.1037/0022-006X.48.5.590

Miller, W. R., Yahne, C. E., Moyers, T. B., Martinez, J., & Pirritano, M. (2004). A randomized trial of methods to help clinicians learn motivational interviewing. Journal of Consulting and Clinical Psychology, 72, 1050-1062.

Moyers, T. B., Martin, T., Houck, J. M., Christopher, P. J., & Tonigan, J. S. (2009). From in- session behaviors to drinking outcomes: A causal chain for motivational interviewing. Journal of Consulting and Clinical Psychology, 77(6), 1113-1124.

Moyers, T. B., Rowell, L. N., Manuel, J. K., Ernst, D., & Houck, J. M. (2016). The Motivational Interviewing Treatment Integrity code (MITI 4): Rationale, preliminary reliability and validity. Journal of Substance Abuse Treatment, 65, 36-42. doi:10.1016/j.jsat. 2016.01.001

Moyers, T. B., & Miller, W. R. (2013). Is low therapist empathy toxic? Psychology of Addictive Behaviors, 27(3), 878-884. doi:10.1037/a0030274

Naar-King, S., & Suarez, M. (2011). Motivational interviewing with adolescents and young adults. New York, NY: Guilford.

Park, M. J., Mulye, T. P., Adams, S., Brindis, C., & Irwin, C. (2006). The health status of young adults in the United States. Journal of Adolescent Health, 29, 305-317.

Patterson, G. R., & Forgatch, M. S. (1985). Therapist behavior as a determinant for client noncompliance: A paradox for the behavior modifier. Journal of Consulting and Clinical Psychology, 53(6), 846-851. doi:10.1037/0022-006X.53.6.846

Peterson, A. V., Kealey, K. A., Mann, S. L., Marek, P. M., Ludman, E. J., Liu, J., & Bricker, J. B. (2009). Group-randomized trial of a proactive, personalized telephone counseling intervention for adolescent smoking cessation. Journal of the National Cancer Institute, 101(20), 1378–1392. doi:10.1093/jnci/djp317

Reinke, K., Herman, K. C., & Sprick, R. (2001). Motivational interviewing for effective classroom management: The classroom check-up. New York, NY: Guilford Press.

Reznicow, K. (2008, April). Motivational interviewing: Applications to child health populations. Paper presented at the Child Health Conference, Miami, FL.

Rogers, C. R. (1965). Client-centered therapy. New York, NY: Houghton Mifflin.

Scholl, M. B., & Schmitt, D. M. (2009). Using motivational interviewing to address college client alcohol abuse. Journal of College Counseling, 12(1), 57-70.

Strait, G. G., Smith, B., McQuillin, S., Terry, J., Swan, S., & Malone, P. S. (2012). A randomized trial of motivational interviewing to improve middle school students' academic performance. Journal of Community Psychology, 40(8), 1032–1039. doi:10.1080/1754730X.2012.736789

Swan, M., Schwartz, S., Berg, B., Walker, D., Stephens, R., & Roffman, R. (2008). The teen marijuana check-up: An in-school protocol for eliciting voluntary self-assessment of marijuana use. Journal of Social Work Practice in the Addictions, 8(3), 284-302.

Terry, J., Smith, B., Strait, G., & McQuillin, S. (2013). Motivational interviewing to improve middle school students' academic performance: A replication study. Journal of Community Psychology, 41(7), 902–909. doi:10.1002/jcop.21574

Terry, J., Strait, G., McQuillin, S., & Smith, B. H. (2014). Dosage effects of motivational interviewing on middle-school students' academic performance: Randomized evaluation of one versus two sessions. Advances in School Mental Health Promotion, 7(1), 62-74. doi:10.1080/1754730X.2013.851995

Tevyah, T. O., Borsari, B., Colby, S. M., & Monti, P. M. (2007). Peer enhancement of a brief motivational intervention with mandated college students. Psychology of Addictive Behaviors, 21(1), 114-119.

The College Board National Office for School Counseling Advocacy. (2011). 2011 National Survey of School Counselors: Counseling at a Crossroads. New York, NY: College Board Advocacy & Policy Center.

Walker, D. D., Roffman, R. A., Stephens, R. S., Wakana, K., Berghuis, J., & Kim, W. (2006). Motivational enhancement therapy for adolescent marijuana users: A preliminary randomized controlled trial. Journal of Consulting and Clinical Psychology, 74(3), 628-632.

West, D. S., Gore, S. A., DiLillo, V., Greene, P. G., & Bursac, Z. (2007). Motivational interviewing improves weight loss in women with Type 2 Diabetes. Diabetes Care, 30(5), 1081–1087. doi:10.2337/dc06-1966.Clinical

Made in the USA
Lexington, KY
20 June 2017